Actually,
It *IS*
Your Parents'
Fault

ALSO BY PHILIP VAN MUNCHING

Boys Will Put You on a Pedestal
(So They Can Look Up Your Skirt):
A Dad's Advice for Daughters

Beer Blast

Actually, It *IS* Your Parents' Fault

Why Your Romantic Relationship Isn't Working, and How to Fix It

Philip Van Munching
and Bernie Katz, Ph.D.

St. Martin's Press
New York

www.stmartins.com

BOOK DESIGN BY AMANDA DEWEY

Library of Congress Cataloging-in-Publication Data

Van Munching, Philip.
    Actually, it *IS* your parents' fault : why your romantic relationship isn't working, and how to fix it / Philip Van Munching and Bernie Katz.—First ed.
        p. cm.
    ISBN-13: 978-0-312-36396-3
    ISBN-10: 0-312-36396-6
    1. Man-woman relationships. 2. Parent and child. I. Katz, Bernie. II. Title.

HQ801.V29 2007
646.7'8—dc22

                                                    2006051185

First Edition: February 2007

10   9   8   7   6   5   4   3   2   1

For Harriet Katz and Elizabeth Auran

Contents

Authors' Note

Because there are two names on the spine of this book, it might seem odd that what follows is written in the first person. A brief explanation: *Actually, It IS Your Parents' Fault* grew out of a series of conversations between two friends, a writer and a therapist. Though we decided early on that the "voice" of the book would be Philip's, both of us contributed to the writing, just as both of us contributed ideas based on observation. (For the record, the technical and theoretical ideas are Bernie's. He is, after all, the one with the Ph.D.) Hopefully, our approach will make what follows conversational, and maybe a little easier to digest than typical coauthored tomes.

Oh, and rest easy if you've ever been a patient of Bernie's or a friend of Philip's: we've changed the name and identifying characteristics of each person who serves as an example on these pages.

The present contains nothing more than the past, and what is found in the effect was already in the cause.

—Henri Bergson, *Creative Evolution*

If it's not one thing, it's your mother.

—Christina Van Munching

Actually,
It *IS*
Your Parents'
Fault

Okay, It's Not *All* Your Parents' Fault

My friend Sara was foolish enough to tell her mother that she had started seeing a therapist to help her work out her relationship problems. "I'll save you a lot of time and money," her mom said, "and I'll tell you what that shrink is ultimately going to say: 'It's all your mother's fault.'" Sara laughed and said, "Come on, Mom, that's such an oversimplification. It's Dad's fault, too, and I'm pretty sure my second-grade teacher deserves some blame as well."

As anyone over the age of twelve knows, there's usually some truth in jest. Sara's mother really *was* worried that her daughter would blame her for all of life's disappointments, and Sara had started to come to the conclusion that most of those disappointments could be traced back to—and pinned on—the people who raised and guided her in her earliest years.

Like many people, Sara approached therapy as a way to find the source of her problems, but basically stopped there. She found things from her childhood that were affecting her as an adult, and she placed some blame—on her mom and dad, that second-grade teacher, and a few of the friends she had in junior high—and then abruptly quit seeing her psychologist. She figured that laying the blame for her unhappiness elsewhere would be enough.

It wasn't. Laying blame may have made her temporarily feel a little better about herself, but it did nothing to help her solve the puzzle of her lousy relationship. Laying blame didn't help her understand *why* she had made the romantic choice she did, or why some of the very things that attracted her to her partner now drove her crazy. Laying blame did exactly zilch in terms of helping her figure out how to fix her relationship . . . or even if the relationship was fixable.

Since blame doesn't seem to fix anything, let's set it aside. Let's leave your parents and friends—in fact, let's even leave your partner—out of our discussion for a bit. Let's talk about *you*. Because I'll tell you right now, just five paragraphs into this book, that the absolute key to the loving relationship you want is understanding the stunningly complex person reading these lines. To reach out to others, you'd first better have a pretty good understanding of yourself.

Quick story: I once had a boss who revered all the silly things he learned in business school, so he was fond of drawing charts and diagrams to explain everything. Those of us who worked for him could expect a drawing or two every week, illustrating department structures, marketing plans . . .

and even our own personalities. I got that last type of drawing from him as a going-away present: I'd tendered my resignation, and my boss wanted to give me a little something to help me with whatever it was I would choose to do next.

He drew a four-paned window, two boxes high and two wide. Above the two panes at the top, he wrote "What others know about you" and "What others don't know about you." Alongside the two panes on the left, he wrote "What you know about you" and "What you don't know about you." Then he filled in each box: "What you know about yourself that others don't," "What both you and others know about you," and so on.

"Now, Philip," he said, "if you take away what you know about yourself, whether other people know it or not, you're left with two things: that which is unknowable about you, and that which other people know about you, but you don't know about yourself. It's that last category that each of us ought to concentrate on. We should learn what others can teach us about ourselves." I resisted the temptation to fill him in on the stuff about himself that all of us in the office knew but couldn't bring ourselves to say—for fear of losing our paychecks—and I thanked him for his four-paned wisdom.

And then years later, I thought about that drawing, and realized that there *was* something interesting to be learned from it . . . if you knew which pane to concentrate on.

There are things about you that no one knows, including yourself. But where my boss was dead wrong was in saying that those things aren't knowable. Just because you're not aware of things that exist within you, deep in your unconscious, doesn't mean that you can't tease them out and learn from them. In fact, doing so is absolutely crucial to understanding both why you're attracted to certain people and why, over time, relationships that start out as blissful and almost carefree can disintegrate into stressful, pain-producing partnerships.

> Just because you're not aware of the things that exist within you, deep in your unconscious, doesn't mean that you can't tease them out and learn from them.

Like most people, you probably believe that you've made love choices—that is, chosen both short-term and long-term romantic partners—largely based on surface stuff such as looks, or a sense of humor, or social acceptability. What you probably haven't realized is that there are all kinds of things going on beneath that surface having to do with the deepest parts of your unconscious. So you may be reacting to an attractive face, but you're also reacting to things deep within *another's* personality that bring out unconscious responses deep within *your* personality. It's those responses, both positive and negative, that can pull you strongly into relationships quite quickly . . . and then pull those relationships apart over time.

The good news is that even though they might seem mysterious, those unconscious responses are really quite predictable, and that predictability can give us clues as to what causes them. Armed with those clues, we can dig into our own personalities, and begin to understand (and change) the things about us that make us attracted to people who aren't really right for us, or that sabotage what should be a stable and loving relationship with someone to whom in most ways we're very well-suited.

Let me introduce you to our guide through all of this, Dr. Bernie Katz. As both a couples therapist and a professor of psychology for the last four decades, Bernie has worked with countless people in various stages of romantic partnership: from couples who are wondering about making a serious commitment to each other to couples who have been married for decades. Through that work, Bernie has encountered just about every relationship woe you can imagine, and several that you probably can't . . . for which you should be very, very grateful.

What Bernie has found, and what we'll cover in the chapters that follow, is that from the very earliest days of *any* romantic relationship, a person can find enough information to predict accurately whether that relationship will ultimately be satisfying or full of conflict. The trick, of course, is knowing what signs to look for . . . and how to read them.

Here's the good news: even if you discover that the signs you got early in your relationship—which, like most folks, you probably ignored—should have sent you packing, it's not too late to turn your conflicted relationship into a happy one. Though my friend Sara refused to get past her blame-laying impulses and into the "Well, how can I use what I've learned constructively?" stage of therapy, it's indeed possible to make changes in yourself that will affect your relationship with your partner for the better. Later on, we'll talk about Bernie's tools for doing just that.

First, though, we're going to talk about *you*. Since personality has everything to do with the success or failure of your relationship, we'll start with how your personality developed. Notice the word *developed?* Contrary to what your great-aunt insisted—"It's amazing; you're just like your grandmother!"— personality is *not* genetic. You're not born with a set of likes and dislikes, strengths and fears. Those things become part of you through a process that takes in all the social complexities you encounter from the moment you're born. So while you may have your father's eyes, there's no way you've had exactly the same experiences he had . . . and there's no way that your personality is exactly the same as his, or anyone else's.

One of the most important parts of your developed personality is your unconscious, home of the stuff that nobody knows about you, *including* you. Most of the questions you have about yourself—even the ones that have nothing to do with your love life, such as "Why can't I stick to a simple diet?" or "I know I have to get this work done, so why am I procrastinating?"—could be answered if only you were able to make your unconscious . . . well, *conscious*. Believe it or not, it's possible to begin to do that, and we'll look at ways you can understand and act on the signals that your unconscious is sending you all the time, in a surprising number of ways. From your dreams to your repeated patterns of behavior, your unconscious has a lot to tell you, and you can learn how to listen.

Then, once you've become more acquainted with your own personality, we'll bring your partner in, and start looking at the notion of "romantic chemistry." We'll see how positive romantic feelings develop . . . and how those feelings are really the reaction of our personality (both conscious and unconscious) to that of our love interest. From there we'll discuss how a romantic relationship grows and changes over time, from the honeymoon stage of "She's the perfect woman!" to the inevitable stage of "Has he *always* been this annoying?" Understanding how conflicts start and grow within a relationship is key to recognizing them in your own—not to mention dealing with them—so we'll go there next. Finally, we'll demystify couples therapy, which is the best option when the work of identifying the problems in your relationship and taking steps to fix them seems overwhelming. As Bernie has told countless couples over the years, when it comes to couples therapy, *you're* not the patient, your relationship is.

> A romantic relationship grows and changes over time, from the honeymoon stage of "She's the perfect woman!" to the inevitable stage of "Has he *always* been this annoying?"

Every relationship has its pitfalls, just like every machine will eventually break down. Forgive me for equating your love affair or your marriage with an automobile, but it's actually a good analogy: if you take proper care of your car, checking the oil and getting to the bottom of those funny noises it sometimes makes, it will most likely run an awfully long time. Ignore the first signs of trouble at your own peril though. Today's tiny puddle on the garage floor is tomorrow's blown engine, you know?

1

Personality . . . or,
How You Became *You*

I f you want to find out what someone knows, you might try handing him a test and a pen to take it with. If you want to find out who someone *is,* you might try flipping that test sheet over, breaking the pen in half, dripping its contents onto the blank page, and asking him what he sees in all that spilled ink.

At least, that was Rorschach's approach.

You've probably heard of Hermann Rorschach, whether you've ever actually taken his famous inkblot test or not. In 1921, Rorschach, a young Swiss psychiatrist, published a series of ten plates, each with random-looking (though, in reality, carefully designed) ink patterns. Some are black ink on a white background, and some have splashes of color added in. The ten plates comprise the Rorschach test, which for more than eight decades has been the subject of endless debate among psychologists.

Theoretically, the test is standardized: everyone given the Rorschach is supposed to be shown the ten plates in the exact same size, order, and facing the same direction. The test-giver is meant to present each without comment and answer any questions a subject might have with a series of prepared answers. In other words, if you take the Rorschach in Davenport, Iowa, and I take it in a little village in Costa Rica, we experience it in exactly the same way.

Which is to say you and I would both be asked to respond to the ten plates in the same order, a certain number of times. Our responses are meant to be completely our own, with no help or encouragement from our respective test-givers. And because there are no right or wrong answers—we are, after all, telling our testers what we "see" in basically random patterns— the standardized way in which we take the test theoretically ensures that our differing reactions to those cards are very telling about us as individuals. (If you see nothing but scary monsters, it's a safe bet you've got a great deal of anxiety, and if I see nothing but genitals . . . well, they might ask the men in the white lab coats to pick me up from the office after the test.)

The thing is, nearly a century after Rorschach gave his first inkblot test, there's still a lot of debate among mental health professionals as to its usefulness. Some argue that it's impossible to "standardize" a test like the Rorschach: how do you account for the effects of location, time of day, the mood of the subject, or how good the tester is at sticking to the test-giving script? If someone takes the inkblot test while experiencing hunger pains, can their results be fairly compared to those of someone who is perfectly comfortable? Others believe that, aside from finding basic areas of obsession, the test isn't reliable in predicting or diagnosing serious psychological disorders. In the eyes of many psychiatrists, psychologists, and therapists, the Rorschach test is so subjective that it proves absolutely nothing.

Which is just plain wrong, as anyone who grew up on *Mister Rogers' Neighborhood* can tell you.

The Rorschach test has, for nearly a century, offered a steady stream of evidence for one psychological fact that is beyond debate: no two human beings are exactly alike, personality-wise. For in all of the tests, given in all of the settings, no two people have ever responded to Hermann Rorschach's smears of ink in exactly the same way. In hundreds of thousands of tests, no two sets of results have ever matched up. Which just proves that Fred Rogers was right when, after putting on his sneakers and sweater at the start of every episode, he assured us that, "There's no one quite like *you*. You're special."

> Fred Rogers was right when, after putting on his sneakers and sweater at the start of every episode, he assured us that, "There's no one quite like *you*. You're special."

You are a unique constellation of thoughts, emotions, behaviors, motives, perceptions, values, and ways of relating to other people. You have your very own history, or "backstory" (as screenwriters like to say), which has distinctive geographical and socioeconomic settings and boasts a colorful cast of characters; namely your parents, siblings, teachers, friends, and so on. All of these circumstances, places, and people are forces that have shaped in you the qualities and traits that collectively make up what's known as your personality. It's that personality of yours, developed almost entirely by early adolesence, that dictates every romantic choice you've made or will make, and that determines much of the course of every relationship you'll ever have, romantic or otherwise.

The reason that your personality is so unique—the same reason you'll never duplicate anyone else's Rorschach test answers—is that no one else has had exactly the same collection of circumstances and experiences as you. Not your parents, not your best friends, not your lovers, not even your siblings. In fact, before we jump into the basic truths Bernie Katz has learned about personality, let's talk about siblings for a moment, and look at the role of "nature" in the nature versus nurture debate as it relates to personality.

I come from a family of eight children, with a ten-year spread between the oldest and youngest. (A little quick math indicates that my mom spent 60 percent of the decade between 1955 and 1965 pregnant. We're still debating whether this means she deserves a medal or a thorough psychological exam.) And in many ways, we're all alike. The children of Peggy and Leo Van Munching, Jr., are all polite: we all hold doors and say "thank you" and offer to sit in the middle seat when on an airplane with a spouse. We all tend toward sarcasm . . . though some try a little too hard (that'd be me) and some can bring down the house almost effortlessly (that'd be my brothers Pieter and Chris). To be sure, there are dozens of other ways in which the eight of us can be used as evidence for the "nature" argument.

Which might mean something if there weren't hundreds of ways in which each of us is completely different from the other seven, and maybe more tellingly, from either of our parents.

Here's the correct, scientifically based response to the person who points to the almost eerie similarities among some siblings over the course of a "nature versus nurture" debate: "Well . . . *duh.*" Of *course* some siblings are very much alike, even beyond their looks and their basic genetic predispositions. Considering that brothers and sisters spend their earliest years sharing many (if not most) circumstances and relationships, there's no surprise that their experiences are comparable. In my family's case, eight kids in ten years makes for some very similar formative experiences: we shared parents and bedrooms and neighborhood kids and hand-me-downs and all of the other things siblings share when they grow up close in age. The key word here is *similar.*

Our experiences, and ultimately our personalities, are never precisely the same as anyone else's though. Even if we share genetic predispositions, as we'll discuss a few pages from now. We may share some common personality traits with friends, and even more with family, but it's inconceivable that anyone on the planet has a personality exactly like ours, for reasons that will become obvious as we explore Bernie's Six Basic Truths About Personality:

1. It's Nurture, Not Nature.
2. Personality Is Experience, Internalized.
3. Your Personality Wasn't Built in a Day.
4. There Are Parts of Your Personality That No One Can See. (Even You.)
5. You Really *Are* "So Predictable."

And

6. Your Personality Determines Your Love Choice.

It's Nurture, Not Nature

Ever spend any time looking through the glass window of a hospital nursery? Because babies tend to be wrapped in the same hospital-issue blankets and sport identical cotton caps, without obvious ethnic differences it can be awfully hard for you or me to tell one baby from the next. It's not so hard for the nurses though. Given several hours with a group of babies, a nurse with any experience can spot different behaviors in even the most recent arrivals to the nursery. For such tiny creatures, it's really remarkable just how different babies can be from one another: they cry differently, eat differently, and even react to noise, light, and touch differently. That's because there are indeed genetic influences that dictate the earliest responses of newborn babies. (Although nurture might play a role in a baby's earliest days as well: some doctors believe that a mother's behavior during pregnancy can actually produce certain responses in her newborn.)

What newborns don't show us, however, are any signs of personality. They're merely showing basic responses brought on by very basic needs: the need to eat, to sleep, to be comforted, to have their diapers changed, and so on. The one common need of all babies at all times is the need to reach out and adapt to the external world: that is, the need to figure out how to get their needs met. Those early responses start to change as infants adapt to the reactions they elicit from parents and caregivers . . . for example, the baby who isn't looked after until his cries become earsplitting wails learns to jump straight to siren-mode when hungry.

From the moment of birth, it's the way in which a parent responds to an infant's needs that serves as the primary influence in the shaping of that child's personality. Notice I didn't say "the degree to which a parent fulfills an infant's needs." No, the key to a child's personality development is found in the personality of the parent: in other words, it isn't just *what* a parent does for a child that shapes that child's personality, it's the *way* a parent does it.

To understand that thought a little more fully, let's back up for a moment and look at the very powerful requirements all children bring with them into the world. There are the obvious physical needs, like food, water, and shelter. The psychological needs of a child, however, are much less obvious. Parenting is often practiced by people who can meet the physical needs of a child, but who haven't much awareness of those psychological needs. In such homes, parenting is shaped by how the child's mother and father were parented, and by all the personality traits—both good and bad—the mother and father possess. Which is swell when the mother and father were raised in nurturing, affectionate, sensitive families . . . but not so swell when the parents that produced the mother and father were self-absorbed, anxious, envious, or emotionally distant.

The psychological needs of children, while not obvious, are really very simple. They need unconditional love, recognition, respect, and need to be related to in ways that will produce positive self-esteem. If a parent treats a child in a way that shows the child is special and important then—*presto!*—the child comes to experience him or herself as special and important. Conversely, if a parent treats a child as though the child is stupid or "useless," the child will grow up feeling stupid and useless, no matter how successful he or she might be in school or in other activities.

From infancy on, a child needs to feel connected to a parent emotionally, perceptually, and cognitively; that is, a child needs the parent to be attuned to the child's feelings and worldview. To feel simpatico with a parent, if you will. When that kind of connection exists—and more important, when a child has that attunement pointed out to her or in any way reinforced ("I know just how you feel, Susie")—she experiences it as love and support. As warmth and gratification. Along with this connection, children need their parents and adult caregivers to perform three basic psychological tasks. First, they need to have their anxiety and distress reduced; they need to feel protected and secure. Second, they need to have appropriate behavioral limits set for them; they need to know what's expected of them so they can be confident that there *is* some order in the world, and that someone is looking out for them.

Third—and here's the biggie—*children need their parents to love them and feel good about them.* If children's main experience is that they are part of a supportive, warm, respectful relationship with their parents, they'll thrive psychologically and physically as well. They'll smile easily, show very little anxiety about strangers, eat and sleep well, and play and learn with enthusiasm.

When those basic psychological needs are not met, because a parent isn't able to create or sustain that connection with a child, you end up with what psychologists call "environmental failure." It's as bad as it sounds: children who are raised in a failed environment—that is, by parents or caregivers who can't fulfill their basic psychological needs—often grow up to be what the world calls "problem children." These are the kids who have a hard time relating to other kids (which can mean they're fearful, tearful, rejecting, or bullying), or who are constantly frustrated, angry, or seem excessively attached to a parent.

> The stuff we're born with is substantially modifiable; the stuff we take in as we're being raised . . . *that's* a lot harder to change.

The real answer to the question of nature versus nurture isn't terribly sexy: your personality is a combination of both . . . but with far more nurture in the stew. Though it's true and well-documented that each of us is born with certain genetic predispositions, it's our upbringing that ultimately determines which of those predispositions are reinforced and which are weeded out of us. The stuff we're born with is substantially modifiable; the stuff we take in as we're being raised . . . *that's* a lot harder to change.

Personality Is Experience, Internalized

The first inkling I ever got about the role a parent plays in developing a child's psyche came on the asphalt basketball court near the parking lot of my elementary school. A kid named Jeff had moved to my hometown a few months before, and all of us in sixth grade found him exotic because he'd lived in or around just about every major city we could think of, including one in Europe. His dad had a job with a company known by its initials—I'll give you a hint, the joke in suburban Connecticut was that the company's initials actually stood for "I've Been Moved"—and, true to the joke, Jeff's family never seemed to stay anywhere for very long. He was a good-enough guy, but he was about as self-critical as it's possible to be at the age of twelve. Even though he was a much better shot than I was on the court, every time he missed, he yelled at himself. "*Man,* I suck!" was a favorite self-critique, as was "God, I'm stinkin' up the court!"

Funny thing was, no matter how bad I was when we played two-on-two as a team, he never got down on me. In fact, he was pretty encouraging. With himself, though, forget about it: he could hit five shots in a row, but if he missed the sixth, you'd have thought he'd just failed his college boards.

One day I found out why.

A bunch of us were asking Jeff about the different cities he'd been to, and my friend Tony asked him if moving so much ever got him confused about where he was living at any given time. Jeff dribbled as he thought about it, took a shot

(which he made), and said, "No, my dad always reminds me."
Tony thought that was funny, but wasn't sure what it meant,
so he asked. "See," Jeff said, "just about every day, my dad tells
me I'm the stupidest kid in . . . and then he says the name of
the town. Right now, I'm the stupidest kid in Darien. Last
year, I was the stupidest kid in Lake Forest." He took another
shot, which he missed, and said, "And I'm the worst damn
shot, too."

Tell a kid like Jeff that he's the stupidest kid in (insert
name of town, here) enough times, and he'll believe it. He'll
become every bit as self-critical as you've been critical of him.
In other words, he'll internalize the experience of being told
that he's stupid. Internalization is the process by which we absorb and take inside ourselves aspects of our external environ-
ments. Such as a parent's constant criticism.

Which is why it's so crucial that a child be raised with
plenty of positive reinforcement, and not only about his intelligence. For instance, a boy who's consistently soothed by a
parent during times of stress—say, after a nightmare or during a thunderstorm—grows up to be an adult with the ability
to soothe himself in stressful situations, often using exactly
the same words he heard as a child. He has an internal soothing mechanism, if you will, built by internalizing the repeated
behavior of his parent. Jeff, on the other hand, probably grew
up to have an internal condemnation mechanism—no matter
how many successful experiences he's had as an adult—
forged during long years as the stupidest kid in Darien, Lake
Forest, Brookline, London, Miami, and so on. . . .

Our inner thoughts, self-perceptions, and the ways we or-
ganize and understand ourselves are in large part variations

and by-products of how our family treated us and reacted to us in our earliest years. And since the older members of our immediate family—that's you, Mom and Dad—already had personalities by the time they raised us, what we're really internalizing are parts of their personalities.

Chances are pretty good that you just had a "gotcha!" moment, reading that last paragraph. "But Philip," you're thinking, "I didn't inherit my parents' personalities at all, because I made a conscious decision to be nothing like them, and rebelled against them every step of the way. The only thing I internalized was the need to be their polar opposite!"

Which could be completely true for you, except that it really isn't. I had the same "gotcha!" moment as Bernie explained personality-as-internalized-experience to me, which prompted Bernie to tell me the following story:

A patient named Rachel had constant battles with her adolescent daughter, Laurie, over Laurie's idea of tidiness. That is, she didn't have one. The clutter in her room was epic; her schoolwork was spread out on her desk as if deposited by a small (but devastating) hurricane. When Bernie asked Rachel why it was so important to her that Laurie clean up after herself, she said, "She's going to be an adult one day. She's going to have a family, a home. Is she going to make her family live in chaos . . . in a messy dump?" Bernie assured her the answer to her question was no, her daughter wouldn't be a messy adult. Laurie had observed her mother's cleaning habits, Bernie told his worried patient, and when the time came for Laurie to assume the responsibilities of an adult she'd unleash her internalized neat freak. "For now," Bernie said, "Laurie *needs* to be a slob at home as a way of proving her independence. It's her way of saying, 'Don't tell me what to do!' " Rachel doubted him completely on the subject, and fretted for years that her daughter was a terminal slob.

And then her daughter left for college in another city. Some five or six weeks into Laurie's freshman year, her mother and father came to visit her in her dorm room, and were only a little surprised to find that Laurie and her roommate had come to such an impasse over tidiness that they'd put a line of tape across the room, effectively splitting it in half. The tape came down one wall, across the floor, up and over the large twin desk, and up the opposite wall. One side of the room was a disaster, with clothes, sheets, food wrappers, and papers taking up just about every square inch of floor, bed, and desk space. The other side was perfectly neat. Clothes were folded up and put away, the bed was made, and papers and books were neatly stacked on the desk.

Rachel, trying not to let her disappointment show too much, looked around the room and said to Laurie, "Well, this is an interesting way of dealing with things." Laurie rolled her eyes. "I know, Mom. It's pretty childish, but . . . my roommate is *such* a pig!" Sure enough, Laurie was the tidy one—she had indeed internalized her mom's cleaning habits—and she went on to complain about her roommate's lack of cleanliness in exactly the same terms that Rachel had used to describe *her* to Bernie.

On a far more serious—and more depressing—note, there is plenty of evidence that the worst behaviors of parents are also often internalized and repeated by their offspring. Even abused children, who grow up swearing to the heavens that they would never turn around and abuse their own kids someday, often follow in their parents' footsteps.

Statistics dishearteningly show that a significant number of abused kids will indeed grow up to be abusers, despite all logic, common sense, and resolve. Blame internalization: upon becoming parents themselves, victims of abuse often find feelings, ideas, and behaviors awakened within them, even when they've sworn that those things are abhorrent. In such instances, having children triggers the internalized behavior, in just about the same way that moving away from home triggered Laurie's internalized neat freak. A little later on, we'll look at how most of the conflict you have with your partner is really triggered, internalized behavior. (In other words, we'll look at how you manage to push each other's buttons, often without even knowing what you've done.)

For four decades, Bernie has taught college courses in abnormal psychology. Each semester, when he gets to the stuff about the process of internalization, he asks his class two questions:

- How many of you have been treated by your parents in such a way that you have sworn to yourself that you would never do the same thing to your child?
- How many of you have watched your parents relating to each other in ways that seem so awful that you make the following vow to yourself: "When I

get married, I will never allow my husband or wife to treat me that way"?

Each and every semester, for forty years, just about every student in every one of Bernie's abnormal psych classes raises his or her hand. To which Bernie responds, "You should live so long." In many of his classes, there are married students, and even students with children of their own. Even though they, too, raised their hands when Bernie posed his questions, they wind up telling stories in class that indicate they already know better: thanks to internalized behavior, the things we swear we'll never do are very often precisely the things we do.

We all carry around a complicated inner world, a world populated by images, thoughts, feelings, and internalized patterns of relating to others that are triggered (become activated) by different life circumstances. Understanding your own inner world—poking around in your past to see why you make the choices you do, and why you behave the way you do—is absolutely essential to understanding, evaluating, and enhancing your relationship with your partner.

Your Personality Wasn't Built in a Day

Thanks to psychologically uninformed—and often just plain lazy—writers, our popular entertainment is filled with stories of people who've had some kind of a "defining moment." These characters have somehow developed long-term patterns of behavior as a result of some single traumatic event in their lives. My favorite example—and let me preface this by saying that in this case, the writer was mocking his fellow screenwriters—comes in the movie *Gremlins.* Late in the film, the character played by Phoebe Cates is asked to explain why she hates Christmas. She solemnly tells the story of how, when she was a little girl, her dad went missing on Christmas Eve, only to be discovered days later, dead in the chimney. (Seems his attempts to be as authentic a Santa as possible went horribly wrong.)

On a less absurd level, we hear stories of defining trauma all the time. It's not uncommon for someone who, because he was bitten by a dog at the age of three, has developed a lifetime phobia of dogs. He believes the bite caused the phobia. In a way, that's absurd, because many people are bitten by dogs and never become phobic around them. Again, we're back to triggers: the youngster who gets bitten and develops a lifelong phobia is more than likely excessively anxious to begin with, and the dog bite serves as an almost accidental stimulus that arouses and makes conscious those anxieties. In other words, the dog bite is the last straw: the anxieties take over in the child, and the child comes to equate dogs with feeling anxious. If the same child were developing with normal and appropriate levels of anxiety, the bite would have caused him to be upset for a few weeks or months around dogs, but certainly wouldn't cause a lifelong phobia.

The point is that we develop our personality as a result of repetitive ways of being related to, and not as a result of a single, isolated experience, except in the most extreme cases. (Like rape, or child abandonment.) If we come from a family where we are often complimented and criticized only rarely, we're not going to develop into self-loathers. However, if, just as my friend Jeff, we come from a family where just about anything we do to try to please our parents is met with criticism (or just plain ignored), it's the repetition of the lousy parenting that becomes internalized. That's what pokes its head out later in life and tells us, "You don't *deserve* to be successful."

Personality develops incrementally, over long stretches of time. Unlike Sigmund Freud, most psychologists today no longer believe that our personality is fully formed by the age of five or six; now it's commonly accepted that personality formation goes on all the way through late adolescence. Still, the earliest years remain critical, for a pretty obvious reason: early experiences come at a time in a child's life when that child is incapable of critical thinking or evaluation. It's all too easy for a child to accept, absorb, and believe that cruel or neglectful parenting is the result of his or her inadequacy or defects. I guarantee that you've never met a young kid who, when criticized by a parent, says, "Wait a minute, I am smart and good and generally pretty adequate. So stop projecting your deficiencies onto me."

A little earlier, I used the example of how a parent helps a child deal with the anxiety caused by a thunderstorm, and it bears repeating: when a mother or father reacts to a child's fear of thunder by being calm and soothing, the child will eventually stop being afraid. Eventually, thunderstorms will be met with awe and fascination by the child, not with anxiety. It's the repetition and consistency of parenting behavior over time that eventually produces behavior patterns in the child that become a permanent part of his or her developing personality.

There Are Parts of Your Personality That No One Can See. (Even You.)

Try to come up with what you ate for dinner last night, and chances are pretty good you can do it. You can also remember your first love, how to play your favorite sport, and what your boss said that got you so angry you nearly quit on the spot. All of these memories are planted in your mind, along with a constant stream of thoughts, beliefs, perceptions, and so on. If you like, think of your mind as a vast storage cabinet, which you can access with remarkable speed and skill. Think about it: you unexpectedly run into someone on the street, and as soon as you see her face you manage to reach into that mind of yours and come up with her name, how you feel about her, and certain memories of her. Your conscious mind is made up of the stuff you know and (mostly) have instant access to.

Your *un*conscious mind, though . . . well, that's a cabinet whose doors have been welded shut. There's plenty in there—memories and thoughts and feelings—but you couldn't pry any of it out with a crowbar. In fact, it's so foreign to you that when things escape from your unconscious and briefly make themselves conscious, you refuse to recognize them as yours.

Think about waking up from a dream. In those first moments of wakefulness, you know what the dream was; chances are you can still imagine the setting, characters, and action pretty vividly. Within moments, though, the details of the dream start to vanish. By the time you've had breakfast, you can't even remember what you dreamed about. That's because your dream has been "repressed," or pushed back out of the realm of your conscious awareness and into your unconscious. (Which makes sense: your unconscious is where your dream came from in the first place.)

Quite naïvely, we believe that the things we do and think aren't influenced by our unconscious. After all, we're not aware of what's lurking in our unconscious, so how often can it really be affecting us? In a word, often. Unconscious motives, thoughts, and ideas push and pull at us constantly, causing us to do things and act in ways that seem baffling to us.

Which is pretty much what therapists spend their days dealing with. People often come to therapists such as Bernie because they're doing something in their life that they don't like and want to stop doing, but they seem unable to. What they want to do is behave rationally and according to logic. Maybe their goal is to stop dating the wrong people or to lose weight; perhaps they want to improve study habits or to stop getting so anxious about things they can't control. Whatever behaviors drive people onto a therapist's couch, chances are pretty good the roots of those behaviors can be found in the patients' unconscious.

Though your conscious and unconscious live in the same neighborhood (your mind), they are essentially lousy neighbors. Your conscious keeps you aware of what you think, what you want, and what you feel. It provides you with a constant road map—your own personal GPS, if you will—of the things you should be doing to achieve your goals, whatever they may be. Your unconscious could not care less about that map; it has absolutely no qualms about steering you off-course. Your unconscious is not interested in your plans, and does not have even a passing relationship with logic. Your unconscious can't be cajoled or persuaded.

And it's precisely that irrational, unconscious, and hidden part of your personality that plays a huge role in your behavior as an adult, and especially in your relationships. Which is why we'll spend the next chapter looking at the sneaky ways in which your unconscious makes itself known to you on a regular basis, and how you can use those signs and signals to your advantage, rather than ignoring them and wishing they'd go away.

You Really *Are* "So Predictable"

Here's why I feel such a kinship with Bernie: we both have to face the Cocktail Party Question. Actually, the problem isn't, "And what do *you* do for a living?" it's the reaction we get when we give our respective answers. See, if you're a lawyer or a store manager or dig ditches or prepare income taxes, people hear your response, nod, and move along. Maybe they ask you a question about your job, but they don't belittle it. Try telling people you're a writer or a psychologist, though, and chances are pretty good you'll want to brain them for what they say next. For me, the response is usually some version of, "Oh, *I'm* going to write a book," as if what I do is the easiest thing in the world. The implication is that if only they weren't busy with real stuff, such as banking, they'd have the time to bang out the Great American Novel . . . *because it's just that simple.*

For Bernie, it's worse: people have absolutely no qualms about telling a therapist—even though he has earned advanced degrees and still spends enormous amounts of time keeping up with the latest advances in his field—about the "problem" with his job. Psychology, they say, is "not an exact science." The snobbery comes from the notion that since psychologists can't measure things to within five decimal points (the standard indication of scientific probability), there's just no relying on the evaluations or predictions that psychologists make. Even in some academic circles, psychology is referred to as a "soft science" that doesn't rate the same prestige and standing as sciences such as physics, chemistry, or biology.

Which is all well and good until a physicist can't figure out why she keeps dating losers, or a biologist needs to stop sabotaging his relationships with his coworkers. That's when the "soft science" doesn't seem so dismissible. In fact, what therapists do is remarkably similar to other scientists: they collect data—in this case through interviews and tests—and create a hypothesis about what drives a given patient's personality. That hypothesis is constantly tested against later data. In fact, after listening to the experiences, dreams, feelings, and irrationalities of a patient for any length of time, most therapists lose their ability to be surprised by just about anything the patient does. Behavior is consistent, reliable . . . and remarkably predictable.

In other words, most of us do the same things again and again and again. And again, for good measure. Some of our actions are good, positive, productive, and helpful, while others can be frustrating, and produce anger or anxiety.

Grace, the forty-year-old divorcée Bernie has had as a patient for some time now, is a great example of the frustrating kind of repetitive, predictable behavior. Not long ago, Grace went to one of those "singles weekends" at a large resort, and found herself in the same ballroom with a few thousand fellow singles. (Think *Sex and the City* on steroids.) All around her, men and women within a few years of her age wandered around the Saturday evening dance, looking for someone they could be interested enough in to start a relationship with. That was the point of being there.

She nursed a drink as she scoped the room, and there—just fleetingly, and from about fifty feet away—she saw a man she thought she'd like to meet. "This is the guy for me," she recalled thinking. After losing him in the crowd, she wandered until she found him again, and sidled up next to him. They ended up talking, and ultimately spending the evening together.

In her next therapy session, Grace told Bernie that the guy was great, and that they'd made plans to see each other again. "And would you believe," she added, "that he's a recovering alcoholic, just like my three ex-husbands?" When Bernie showed absolutely no surprise, Grace got a little annoyed. "Come on," she said, "you aren't shocked at all by what I'm telling you?" Bernie told her he wasn't. "For you," he said, "romantic chemistry seems to be elicited by people who have a personality pattern associated with large amounts of alcohol." (Which was a nice way of telling her that her repeated experiences showed she was only drawn to drunks.)

> We all pick the same kinds of people over and over; we enter into similar kinds of relationships again and again.

Grace's love life is a great example of reliable, consistent behavior. We all pick the same kinds of people over and over; we enter into similar kinds of relationships again and again. If we're jealous and possessive in one relationship, it's a safe bet we'll be jealous and possessive in our other relationships. If we're honest, open, and trusting in one relationship, those tend to be qualities found in our other relationships. In other words, we're all guilty of what Freud called the repetition compulsion; we have an unconscious need to repeat certain behaviors. *But*—and here's the good part—if we can make those unconscious needs known to us, we gain a remarkably powerful tool for evaluating the romantic choices we make. We learn to predict the types of people we choose, to understand why we choose them, and to anticipate the potential problems in our relationships.

Your Personality Determines Your Love Choice

By the time we reach adulthood, almost all of us have had the experience of being attracted to or even falling in love with someone else. For some of us, that experience seems to occur weekly. Inevitably, at some point early on in each attraction or relationship, we wonder what it is, exactly, about the other person that we are attracted to. (Actually, that can happen late in a relationship, as well, but in a negative way: "What did I *ever* see in him?") Whenever the question of what attracted us comes up, we tend to answer it in physical terms; we consider looks, build, body language, and the like. Maybe we go with one or two of the traditional old saws such as "He made me laugh" or "She seems like such a kind person."

It's rare, though, that we turn our attention around and think in terms of what it is about *us* that makes the object of our affection so attractive and desirable. In other words, we don't ask ourselves the single most relevant question when it comes to figuring out the origin of our longing for someone else: *What does the personality trait I seem to be so drawn to in others reveal about* me?

Grace's story—her predictable attraction to men who are recovering alcoholics—shows not only the repetitive nature of personality, but also points out the roots of romantic attraction: the man she met at the singles weekend had the personality trait she required in order to find him attractive. "Ah," but I hear you protest, "she couldn't possibly have known that he was a recovering alcoholic when she first spotted him, fifty feet away!" According to her story, it was only after she'd sidled up to him in an extremely crowded room, and after they'd established mutual attraction, that their conversation turned to his past and she learned he was a recovering alcoholic, just like her three ex-husbands. And you're right, of course. Consciously, she couldn't have known.

And yet the remarkable level of coincidence suggests that in a way, she did know. She knew it *unconsciously*.

Let's call it intuition . . . but not "women's intuition," because both genders intuit things about people we've just met. Long before we consciously "know" anything about them, we're able to form some level of attraction to a face across a room or a blind date. We're able to make a (remarkably accurate) assessment of the friendship potential in a new coworker. In fact, the initial moments of meeting a potential partner can stir up a wide variety of responses within us, from disappointment to neutrality to attraction. Those responses aren't random, but rather determined by an instant—though unconscious—recognition of personality traits that the other person has.

Take Len, for example. Like many forty-year-old single men living in a big city, Len went out to bars, parties, and did all the other stuff one does when you're looking for a partner. And, pretty regularly, he had the same experience: he became attracted to a woman, introduced himself, and embarked on a long conversation with her, often lasting several hours. By the end of that first conversation, he always found—to his dismay—that his new interest was a cold, emotionally distant, and self-absorbed person. His initial attraction evaporated. It's important to add that these women came in different shapes and sizes: our friend Len wasn't drawn to them because they all fit some physical "type" that aroused him.

After several years of therapy with Bernie, Len came to understand and accept that he'd never, in fact, been attracted to any other type of woman, personality-wise. He found it no coincidence that he had always seen his mother as cold, emotionally distant, and self-absorbed.

One of the great contradictions of our psychological existence is that we tend to become attracted to people with personality traits for which we claim conscious disdain. While we're happy to announce to the world that there's a certain type of person with whom we'd like to get romantically involved, the reality is that we consistently "fall for" people who not only lack the qualities that would make them our "type," but also have the traits we think we're running away from. The disconnect between what we say we're looking for and the traits our partners actually possess is easily explained: our conscious desires can be *very* different from our unconscious needs.

In his many years as a teacher and counselor of college students, Bernie has noticed a pattern. (I've found the same pattern in my many years of being the guy whose female friends call him for advice on their love lives.) It goes like this: a young woman will complain that her boyfriend treats her badly. He doesn't call when he says he will, he breaks dates at the last minute, maybe he even puts her down in front of her friends. After agonizing over it and talking to all of her friends about it, she dumps the guy, and promptly meets a man who treats her much more thoughtfully. Phone calls, flowers, he's a good listener . . . the whole nine.

Which is all well and good for a week or two, at which point she realizes that she just isn't attracted to the new guy; she finds their budding relationship "boring." Which suggests to Bernie that, no matter what she says consciously, the young woman is *unconsciously* seeking out men who will treat her badly.

Like many people, Len found himself very attracted to people who would ultimately hurt and disappoint him, and far less attracted (or not at all attracted) to the type of person who could provide him with the loving, supportive relationship he professed to want. If you're like Len, there are two solutions to your conflict:

1. Become romantically involved with someone to whom you're not powerfully attracted.

Or

2. Change your personality, which will change the type of person to whom you'll be attracted.

Len chose the former, and is now married to a woman whom he loves and respects, but who doesn't turn him on like the cold, emotionally distant, self-absorbed girlfriends of old. The second solution was chosen by another patient of Bernie's, a young woman in the middle of studying for an advanced degree. Beautiful, smart, and accomplished at the age of twenty-five, she kept finding herself attracted to—and a few times almost married to—men with little apparent ambition, who almost seemed to pride themselves on their lack of education and lousy prospects. In other words, she always went for losers. After realizing (and eliminating) the unconscious belief that she was somehow inadequate, she started to find herself attracted to men who were more her equal in terms of intelligence and achievement.

When it comes to choosing a partner, the conscious and unconscious aspects of your personality are locked in a constant turf war . . . and your unconscious fights dirty. To get its needs met, the part of your personality that you aren't aware of will ignore what's good for you, spit in the face of what's rational, and will often sabotage your happiness. To fight back, and be capable of having the relationship you want with the person who's right for you, you're first going to have to travel into your own psychological makeup, and get a little better acquainted with that unconscious of yours.

Bring a flashlight.

Since Relationships Can Test You, It Helps to Take Good Notes

Before we go on, I'd like to suggest that you get yourself a notebook. Nothing fancy; just something large enough to make writing comfortable, and something that will fit more than twelve words on a page. (In other words, don't buy one of those wire-bound, fits-in-your-pocket things at your local office supply store. They're a pain to write in.)

Over the chapters that follow, Bernie and I will give you lots of opportunities to take notes—if you're so inclined—on what we think you'll find to be a fascinating subject: you. We'll have you make self-observations and write down memories. You'll collect data. You'll answer questions about where you've been, romantically speaking, and you'll describe where you are now. Ultimately, you'll use your notes to get a much better understanding of *you;* an understanding that will help you find the love you want, or fix the one you've got.*

So get that notebook. Don't worry about me; I'll wait.

---

* Which, incidentally, was one of my first title ideas for this book. Until I looked on the self-help shelf in my local bookstore and found that Dr. Phil beat me to it. *Damn,* that guy is good.

2.

Digging Into Your
Unconscious Mind

In just about every horror movie I saw as a kid, there was a
scene where some fool decides it's best to go searching for
the killer/ghost/boogeyman in the basement. In the dark,
armed with only a flashlight, he or she creeps down the stairs.
There's a scream, followed by a thud or slashing noise, and we
cut to the people who were too smart to go down that creaky
wooden staircase, now huddled together in the kitchen, quak-
ing with fear at the new and terrible silence.

As a kid, I remember vividly my feeling of superiority to
the dummy who just got himself killed: *I'd* never be so stupid
as to go down into the basement. Basements are scary.

If your mind is a house—one that, unlike the average
New York apartment, is filled with closet space—your unconscious mind is the basement. It was Sigmund Freud who introduced us to the idea that the thoughts, emotions, and

memories we find too upsetting to cope with are pushed into the unconscious mind. By repressing the most upsetting things on our minds—rendering them unconscious—we're able to stay on an even psychological keel.

The problem, of course, is that the bad things—like those movie monsters—are awfully hard to keep down. The contents of our unconscious minds don't lie dormant, but rather creep back into our daily lives in unexpected ways. Think of it this way: ever try holding an air-filled ball underwater? The water pressure surrounding the ball keeps forcing it toward the surface, which means you have to create your own pressure to keep it down. Your mind does the same thing with your unconscious in that it expends a steady stream of psychic pressure to keep things buried that would upset you if they were to surface, or become conscious. The difference, of course, is that (in my analogy) you're only holding one ball down, and your mind has all kinds of things to keep under the surface.

So maybe that ball underwater analogy should be sharpened. Imagine instead trying to hold a large number of small air-filled balls underwater. You'd have to be creative, and use your arms, legs, and torso to block those balls from rising . . . and, of course, you'd be at least somewhat unsuccessful: some of them would find a way up. But while those balls would be immediately recognizable on the surface, the stuff that bubbles up from your unconscious often comes out in ways that make it difficult to know just what you're seeing . . . so you're left with odd, unexplainable, and often irrational occurrences in your life, caused by feelings that are still *mostly* unconscious. We'll get to just what types of occurrences qualify as signs of the unconscious mind in a moment, but first let's talk about the mind as a whole.

We're all born into an interpersonal world: our memories, thoughts, and feelings almost always involve some element of our relationships with others . . . and since our parents and siblings comprise our earliest and most formative relationships, it's those family bonds that loom largest in our developing psyche. We internalize (bring inside of ourselves) the consistent and repetitive stuff that we experience through our family. For example, the child whose mother reliably soothes her with a few comforting phrases during thunderstorms will eventually learn to soothe herself with those same words. Likewise, a baby who is always shushed by an angry father will grow into a child who lives in fear of any commotion that will bring out his dad's wrath. These are examples of internalized experience.

Our collection of internalized experience is the central part of our personality, which is really our permanent psychological structure, the engine that drives all of our behavior. Those aspects of our relationships with others that are gratifying, rewarding, or in some way meet our developmental needs, we keep at the ready in our conscious mind along with other positive thoughts, feelings, and memories. (In other words, we keep them in the house sitting atop that scary basement.)

When a repetitive interpersonal pattern is upsetting, though, it can be tossed into the unconscious, where we don't have to look at it. Think of the unconscious as the mind's self-preservation mechanism; since too much anxiety can drive you "out of your mind," your mind relieves some of your anxiety by storing much of its upsetting content in the unconscious, where it will no longer directly bother you.

Unfortunately, that bad stuff will still *indirectly* bother you. That's why the child who has long forgotten his father's angry shushing grows into an adult who can't stand loud noises: the noises themselves aren't the problem, it's the re-pressed memory of the father's anger that causes the discom-fort. It's important to remember that even though your mind has rendered something unconscious, that something is still very much present (though maybe not accounted for), and still an important building block of your personality. And since we know that your developed personality has everything to do with how you make romantic choices, your unconscious can wreak havoc with your love life.

That's why it's so critical to be able to step back, psycho-logically speaking, and try to recognize some of the methods by which your unconscious reveals itself to you. The more you know about your *whole* mind, the more control you can exer-cise over every aspect of your life. Stepping back and observ-ing your unconscious mind at work allows you to evaluate experiences and relationships . . . and figure out how you *really* feel about the people in your life, especially your partner.

I know, I know: how on earth do you step back and ob-serve something you can't see, and of which you are not con-sciously aware? Since it isn't possible to recognize unconscious thoughts while they're hidden in the darkest recesses of your mind, you have to do what the police do when a criminal is hiding in a dark building: guard the exits and wait. Since things bubble up out of your unconscious all the time, you won't have to wait long, as long as you have the "exit doors" of your mind covered. So here they are, the five main ways your unconscious becomes fleetingly conscious, and gives you clues to aspects of your personality that you probably aren't aware of. The five "exit doors" we'll look at are:

1. Dreams
2. Freudian Slips
3. Emotional Overreactions
4. Repetitive Behavior Patterns
5. Symptoms

Dreams

Using the scenes that play through your head in your sleep isn't exactly a new way to search for self-understanding. As Sigmund Freud wrote more than a century ago, "the interpretation of dreams is the royal road to a knowledge of the unconscious activities of the mind." Looked at properly, every dream you have is an encoded message from the depths of your unconscious, looking to tell you something consciously.

Before we get into how to interpret—or decode—the content of dreams, though, let's take a look at the aspects of dreaming that we all share. Starting with the fact that we *all* dream. And not only do we all dream, but we all have several dreams per sleeping cycle . . . very few of which we manage to remember. (When someone tells you "Oh, I never dream," they're wrong, as sleep research centers have proven. What they're really saying is "I never remember my dreams," which is certainly possible, given the ephemeral nature of dreaming.) So we all dream, and most of our dreams have a tendency to disappear very quickly. The third common aspect of dreaming is that the content of any given dream has the habit of being, well, *nutty:* it makes no sense to us, and often flouts the laws of time, space, and physical reality.

That nuttiness, coupled with the fact that dreams tend to slip away from memory within moments of waking, certainly make it seem like dreams aren't *meant* for interpretation. How can it be possible to interpret a dream where you fly, or talk to a long-dead relative, or grow a second head? It all seems too crazy and fleeting to have any meaning.

Well, there's your conscious mind again, doing its best to force the stuff that's bubbled to the surface back down into the unconscious mind. The truth is, even the craziest, most nonsensical dreams are windows of opportunity, giving us a rare chance to learn something about ourselves . . . some of which we'll experience as enlightening and helpful, and some of which we may very well find distressing, and even challenging to our most basic self-assumptions. Dreams quite often contradict thoughts and perceptions that we consciously "know" to be true.

During her first three sessions as a patient of Bernie's, a woman named Diane repeatedly told him that she found him to be warm, caring, sensitive, accepting, and responsive; in other words, she came in each week with an extremely positive feeling about the man she had chosen as a therapist. "I know we're a good fit, and you'll be able to help me with my problems," she told him. At the start of her fourth session, Diane seemed agitated and confused. When Bernie asked what was wrong, she launched into the story of a dream she had had a few nights before, and remembered vividly:

"I was coming to your office for a session, and there was a blinding snowstorm," she said. "I pulled my car up to the curb, and could barely get the door open because the wind was so strong. I tried to walk up the driveway to the office door, but the wind was pushing against me and the snow and ice were starting to cover me. As hard as I fought to make it to the door, I couldn't . . . and I started to worry that I'd freeze to death. I could see you, standing in the doorway, watching me with a smile on your face."

So much for her feeling that Bernie would be helpful, huh? This is why Diane was so confused and agitated: in the dream, she saw Bernie as the exact *opposite* of what she kept telling him he was in their sessions. But rather than let her dismiss the dream as bizarre and nonsensical, Bernie encouraged her to use it as an opportunity to listen to her unconscious. Working together, they didn't need an elaborate decoding device to figure out what the imagery of the dream was saying to her:

What Diane was *feeling* in her dream was *cold* and *frustrated*.

The dream featured an opposing force—the wind—which represented a conflict.

Contrary to the way she consciously thought about her therapist, in the dream he was completely unhelpful.

Clearly, it was time for Diane to ask herself some questions about how she really felt about Bernie. Why would her unconscious tell her he was uncaring when she had been regularly announcing that he was warm and helpful? (The dream made her realize just how odd it was that she had *immediately* started declaring positive feelings for him.) The dichotomy suggested an answer: maybe there was a reason she had to immediately see him as caring . . . and maybe that was something she'd been experiencing in other relationships.

That's an important thing to realize when interpreting your dreams: they're not always *only* about the people who pop up in them, they can also tell you a great deal about your patterns of relating to people. In Diane's case, a lengthy discussion of the snowstorm dream revealed that she had a long history of convincing herself that others were caring and helpful when in fact she found herself angry with them. She would reject (cast into her unconscious) her feelings of anger toward other people by burying those feelings under layers of compliments. Because of the unconscious anger, though, her relationships were mostly dissatisfying and frustrating.

From all we've discussed so far, I'm sure you can guess that Diane's relationship problems were rooted in what she'd experienced as a child. From an early age, she had witnessed her parents' inability to handle anger in any productive way—they tended to run away from people and situations that made them angry—and she started equating anger with rejection. She internalized how her parents reacted to conflict, and so she grew up needing to deny any feelings of anger she was having toward others (especially boyfriends) out of fear that her anger would spell the end of any relationship.

Bestowing lavish compliments on others was her way of preserving relationships . . . and avoiding rejection. "After all," she told Bernie, "a lousy relationship is better than no relationship."

Ultimately, Diane was able to tell Bernie what he had said in their very first session that had angered her . . . and she was shocked when her expression of anger didn't end their relationship. If not for her dream about the snowstorm, it's quite possible that Diane and Bernie would have had a short, unsatisfying doctor-patient relationship.

Bernie fared a little better in the recurring dream of a forty-year-old patient named Rachel, who had come to him out of frustration that she had been in a string of relationships where the men were never sensitive enough to meet her needs. "In the dream," she said, "I'm in a large house, and I'm surrounded by people from every stage of my life; my parents, my siblings, my friends, and even some old boyfriends. One at a time, they try to tell me about all of my good points. But as soon as each of them starts speaking, I begin to yell at them, telling them that they don't know what they're talking about. Suddenly," she told Bernie, "*you* step forward, but before you can even speak, I gently shush you and push you away."

Rachel had taken the dream to mean that she was terribly insecure, which was certainly true, but not nearly all that the dream was telling her. She hadn't thought about what the images in the dream had to say about the *other* people in her life, especially those "insensitive" men with whom she was having so much trouble. In discussing her dream with Bernie, it became clear to her that her disappointment with men was largely of her own making: though she wasn't exactly yelling at boyfriends when they would say something nice about her, she *was* often behaving in such a way that would make them angry and uncertain of her interest in them. When they would complain, and tell her that they were feeling rejected, she would find them disappointing and unacceptable. (Her treatment of Bernie in the dream—shushing him instead of yelling at him—meant that their relationship was one she wanted to spare from her usual rejection-disappointment pattern.) Rachel and Bernie, in the months that followed, examined why Rachel would act unconsciously in ways to bring about the very breakups that she consciously dreaded. The important part of the story for us is that it was her dream that made her aware of what she was unconsciously doing to sabotage her romantic relationships.

Dreams work the same way for people who have been in long-term relationships, of course. The Brodys came to Bernie for couples therapy because of a conflict they'd been having for almost a decade. Their trouble started when Stan Brody took a job that put him on the road a great deal. From the outset of his traveling, Sue Brody wanted to know every detail of her husband's itinerary, which made Stan feel controlled and distrusted. He reacted by refusing to tell her exactly where he'd be at any given time, which in turn made his wife angry. (And distrusting. And sexually withholding.) Eventually they sought help.

Early on in their therapy, Sue talked about a dream in which she found herself standing on a ledge of the Empire State Building. "It's a high floor, and the ledge is very small and precarious. Looking downtown, I can see a huge tidal wave coming, and I'm praying that I'm high enough so that I won't get washed away," she said. "The wave crashes against the side of the building, and I get all wet. It keeps crashing and crashing against the building, and the ledge is getting slippery, and I feel like I'm going to get pulled into the water. Suddenly, I wake up, terrified."

Stan was stunned. "Obviously," he said, "there's something in your life that seems terrifying to you; so what is it?" He was even more stunned to learn that *he* was the Empire State Building in her dream . . . and that she felt overwhelmed and terrified by his refusal to tell her where he would be at any given point in his travels. In therapy, the Brodys learned that as a young girl, Sue's family dynamic had been one of abandonment: in times of psychological need, her parents would consistently walk away from her. They also realized that Stan had grown up with a controlling mother . . . and was, on an unconscious level, responding angrily to *her* whenever Sue asked about his plans.

When Stan realized that he could help his wife overcome her severe anxiety simply by giving her an itinerary, he was able to let go of his fear of being controlled. The dream also helped to make each of the Brodys aware of basic themes in their respective relationships with others . . . that is, it showed Stan that he had long dreaded the feeling of being controlled by women, and Sue became consciously aware of the abandonment fears that had complicated her entire romantic history.

Even though it can seem crazy and mysterious, dream material is always a source of information, and can be quite revealing about the dreamer. The trick to getting at that information is twofold: first you have to *remember* the dream, then you have to *interpret* it.

Oddly enough, most people seem to have a harder time with remembering than they do with interpreting. While it's true that some folks have no trouble repeating the content of their nocturnal ramblings in terrific detail, for most of us, dreams start to disappear back into our unconscious somewhere between opening our eyes and brushing our teeth. That's a gradual process: upon awakening, we remember far more detail than we do just minutes later. By lunchtime, we might recall some goofy aspect about a dream, or the identity of the person we were dreaming about, but by then the details have become too hazy to be useful.

So unless you're one of those lucky few who remember their dreams, you're going to have to find a way to commit your dream material to memory. There are two basic ways to do that. One way is to tell your partner (or roommate, or anyone else who's handy) about your dream as soon as you wake up, because repeating the details helps cement them in your memory. Unfortunately, the "oral tradition" method of dream retention is problematic for a number of reasons. You may not have anyone handy . . . or anyone handy who happens to be *awake*. You may not want to tell the person you *do* have handy what you've been dreaming about, for fear of upsetting or offending them. (Or for fear they'll start hiding the sharp objects in the house.) But even if you have a person handy who is awake and not easily offended or upset, the practical problem with repeating your dreams is that it's quite an imposition to constantly burden someone else with the stories your unconscious tells you in your sleep.

Which is why using that journal I've encouraged you to start and *writing your dreams down* is a much more effective method of remembering them. Keeping paper and pen next to your bed allows you to commit a dream to memory no matter what time you awaken from it, and it provides a much more permanent record of the dream. (That's another pitfall of repeating your dreams verbally to another: just because you got them out of your mouth once doesn't mean you'll remember them days or weeks later.) I remember reading years ago that one of my favorite pop stars, Sting, keeps a pad on his bedside table to record his dreams . . . and actually named his first solo album—*The Dream of the Blue Turtles*—after one of them.

With notes in hand, you can begin the work of sussing out what your dreams are trying to tell you. The trick is to look at the *entire* dream as if it's a movie. Recognize that it has a setting and characters, and even if the actions of the people in the dream seem completely odd, your dream has a plot as well. With all of these things in mind, try to answer these questions about different aspects of your dream in your journal:

1. How am I interacting with people in the dream, or how are they interacting with each other?
2. What emotional state is present in the dream: excitement, anxiety, anger, sadness, something else? If I can't tell *how* the people in the dream are feeling emotionally, is there something in the imagery that suggests any type of feeling, such as extreme cold, or danger, or confusing action?

3. Is there an action or feeling in the dream that flies in the face of what I feel when I'm awake? (Am I angry with someone in the dream who I normally get along very well with?)
4. Is there some action or feeling that seems completely unlike what I usually do or feel?
5. What do I consciously think of the people who appear in the dream?

When looking for information about yourself in your dreams, it helps to start with a very basic assumption: all aspects of a dream are aspects of *you*. The people, the imagery, the relationships, and even the actions that make up your dream all point to the many (and varied) internal experiences that make up your personality . . . and because that personality is so complex, your dreams can be quite complex, too. Like this dream, which newly remarried Matt told to Bernie: "I'm in my house, about to leave on vacation," Matt said. "There's a man in the house, but I don't know him. He tells me that vacations are extravagant and unnecessary, and that they're taken by selfish, arrogant people. Suddenly, I find myself in a dingy-looking cafeteria—like a soup kitchen—and I'm serving food to poor people."

There are a number of things going on in Matt's dream, and each aspect reflects a part of his personality:

- I'm about to go on vacation. (Matt wants to enjoy life; to do pleasurable things.)
- The man tells me that vacations are extravagant and for the arrogant. (Matt feels others will judge him for enjoying himself.)

- I'm serving food to poor people. (Matt feels that service to others is better than serving his own desires.)
- I'm in a dingy-looking cafeteria. (Matt's self-esteem drops because he has given in and denied himself the pleasure of a vacation.)

Matt, it's not hard to figure out, had an unconscious struggle going on within himself between the desire to do for himself and the obligation to do for others. Clearly, he felt that the latter need—doing for others—in some way always trumped his own desires. In his second marriage, he'd come to see anything he did for himself as somehow taking away from the other members of his new family. If he bought himself nice clothes, for example, he felt like he was "robbing" his wife and stepchildren. By realizing his unconscious feelings about his new obligations, and discussing them with his wife, Matt became less anxious almost immediately . . . and that judgmental stranger disappeared from his dreams.

Your dreams have a tremendous amount to tell you about your relationships: your innermost thoughts—the ones that often unconsciously guide your behavior toward your parents, your friends, and your partners—are often revealed to you in your sleep. But teasing those feelings out and making note of them isn't enough: you have to actually use your new knowledge to make your relationships more productive and satisfying. Bernie recalls the story of a young patient who came to him because of severe anxiety attacks during which she thought she was slowly disappearing. One day she told him of a dream about a little girl trying desperately to talk to her family members, only to have them respond in a crazy language she couldn't understand. Though Bernie recognized that the noncommunicative characters in her dream represented her family members as they really were, she was so invested in her belief that her parents and siblings were actually helpful and attentive that she refused for a long time to see what her unconscious was trying to tell her.

Over the course of her therapy, the young woman started to reveal—and consciously realize—that her family communicated very poorly with her. They would assume knowledge of things that she didn't actually have, and would give her information without context or explanation, leaving her frightened and confused. (Imagine signing up for an introductory course in an academic subject and accidentally walking in to the advanced, graduate-level lecture instead. That's what she felt like almost every day.) Worried that there was something wrong with her, she started having panic attacks and odd dreams. Once her therapy emboldened her to talk to her family about her constant confusion, her panic attacks decreased.

If you find yourself having nightmares—or even just repetitive dreams—about your partner, you need to recognize that your relationship is causing you stress or anxiety. To help you decode such dreams, try discussing them with your partner. Not only will you get the benefit of their reaction and insight, you'll stimulate your own thinking. Remember, of course, that dreams are about the dreamer, and you need to keep the focus of any discussion about your dreams on *you*. On *your* feelings and anxieties. Keep in mind that they're not guilty of the things they've done in your dreams, so being angry with your partner isn't appropriate. If you make your partner feel comfortable that you're looking at your dreams as a way to make your relationship better, you can avoid adding even *more* stress to your relationship. And don't worry so much about upsetting them: if your relationship is a worthy one, they'll want to know if they're causing you anxiety in some way, and they'll want to help ease that anxiety.

Freudian Slips

When I was in college, the game show *Wheel of Fortune* held tryouts in Chicago. Not the most detail-oriented guy, I missed the part in the announcement about the different times for the (sparsely populated) college tryouts and the general public tryouts, and so I found myself in a proverbial cattle call: hundreds and hundreds of *Wheel* addicts, packed into a hotel banquet room, each ready to scream "Big money!" like an idiot in the hopes of impressing the *Wheel* producers.

First, those producers whittled down our numbers based on answers we had given in our personal questionnaires, and then they thinned our ranks further by giving us a written quiz. When I was identified as a finalist, and asked to stay long enough to play a mock round of *Wheel of Fortune,* my college student cool departed for points unknown, and I became just another screaming, cheering fool.

When my turn to play came, I became a fool of an entirely different sort. In case you're not familiar with *Wheel,* it's basically the kids' game Hangman crosspollinated with roulette.

You're shown a series of blank spaces that represent the letters in a phrase, you spin a wheel, and if you correctly guess a letter that appears in the phrase, you win the dollar amount indicated by your spin, and your turn continues. By the time my turn came around, other players had revealed several letters of the puzzle we were trying to solve: L_ke __ther, l_ke s_n. Slam-dunk time, I figured. I'd spin, ask for the last remaining consonant, and solve the puzzle. I spun, screaming "Big money!" with all the enthusiasm in the world. The producers smiled at me as I landed on $1,000.

"Give me an *m!*" I shouted. The producers stopped smiling. The people on either side of me seemed to shrink away. As the next person spun the wheel, I realized my mistake: the phrase was "Like *fa*ther, like son," not "Like *mo*ther, like son."

Paging Dr. Rex, Dr. Oedipus Rex . . .

For years, I was convinced that I'd made a horrible oedipal slip, and revealed myself to be some kind of a pervert with a thing for mom. Turns out instead that I'd simply made a Freudian slip, and revealed a very real truth about myself. The puzzle, after all, was an equation (*a* is like *b*), not a love letter, and deep down I must have felt that temperamentally I'm a lot more like my mom than I am like my dad. At the *Wheel of Fortune* tryouts, my unconscious let me—and several dozen total strangers—in on that secret.

Maybe the most remarkable thing about the Freudian slip is the refusal of most folks to believe it has any meaning. They convince themselves that a slip is just an accident, a chance remark that comes out of nowhere. In fact, people often refer to a Freudian slip as "a slip of the tongue," and they're often not even aware they've made one. "Where did *that* come from," they'll tell you, embarrassed, when you point their slip out to them. If the slip has a negative (or downright nasty) connotation, they'll deny vehemently that they meant anything by it.

Years ago, a young woman told Bernie of just such a slip. "I was dating a nice guy named Bob," she said. "I had met someone else I was much more interested in, but I didn't act on it for fear of hurting Bob's feelings. I didn't want to date him anymore, but how could I tell him? When he called one night, I couldn't believe it when I picked up the phone and said, 'Hi, *Blob.*'" (Imagine what she would have said if she *did* want to hurt his feelings!) Bob, of course, got angry, and accused her of accidentally telling him what she really felt about him. Though she protested, he refused to listen and instead broke up with her. Amazingly, her unconscious slip caused her boyfriend to correctly guess what the situation was, and to take the action that *she* wanted to take, but was incapable of.

Other examples from Bernie's practice are just as effective in demonstrating the connection between the unconscious and the Freudian slip, like the story of Abigail, whose name matched her poised demeanor. She arrived at his office at exactly the agreed-upon minute, meticulously dressed and groomed, and spoke with the deliberateness of a perfectionist. She had sought therapy because her family doctor recognized her stomach pain as anxiety-based. When asked what she thought was causing her anxiety, she told Bernie, "I'm not sure, but I guess it has to do with my husband and our relation*shit*." It doesn't take a shrink to know that her guess was right on.

> When asked what she thought was causing her anxiety, she told Bernie, "I'm not sure, but I guess it has to do with my husband and our relation*shit*."

Likewise, a divorced man named Howard, who came to Bernie after the breakup of a long-term love affair, revealed his true feelings with a slip. Though he normally dealt with his anger and depression by insisting that everything was all right and he was doing fine, one day when he meant to tell his therapist that "everything is falling into place," he said instead that "everything is falling into *pieces*."

Another patient, Wes, made a telling Freudian slip *while* discussing his tendency to suppress his most unhappy thoughts. Wes's sessions with Bernie followed a typical pattern: Wes would start with a laundry list of complaints about the terrible situations in his life, and he'd express despair over the idea that "Nothing's going to change; nothing's going to get better." Suddenly, though, he would completely shift gears, and start declaring that things weren't so bad and were actually getting better. Finally, Bernie pointed out to Wes that he seemed frightened by his negative feelings and was protecting himself by suddenly becoming overly optimistic. Wes denied that he was *ever* a pessimistic person: "You're so wrong about me," he said. "I've always been a very positive thinker. In fact, my motto is *'Every silver lining has a cloud.'*" Funny how at the exact moment it was being most forcefully denied, Wes's unconscious found a way to assert itself.

People don't just make Freudian slips in front of their partners and therapists, however: sometimes the whole country is tuned in. Take the case of President Nixon, who at the height of the Watergate scandal that would eventually end his presidency, decided to give a televised policy speech. He intended to completely ignore Watergate, and give the American people the sense that their president was hard at work on things that were important to them, and not rendered ineffective by the swirling scandal. In addressing the problems of the public assistance program, he *meant* to say, "Join me in a new effort to replace the discredited *present* welfare system." What he *did* say, instead, was, "Join me in a new effort to replace the discredited *president*." Even the president isn't immune to unconscious forces.

I shared my *Wheel of Fortune* story with Bernie, who laughed and told me a story of his own, about an instance where Oedipus and Freud *really* collided. While teaching his course in abnormal psychology, Bernie was discussing Freud's theory of the Oedipus complex, in which a child develops an erotic attraction to the parent of the opposite sex. One student became so annoyed at what he saw as the total absurdity of such an idea that he raised his hand to comment. What he meant to say to the class was, "Do you mean that a small child can actually become seductive with his opposite-sexed parent?" but in his agitation, it came out as "Do you mean that a small child can actually become seductive with his *oversexed* parent?"

Now *there's* a guy with mother issues.

For a therapist dealing with patients' anxieties on a daily basis, Freudian slips are uncommonly helpful as clues to what's going on in a patient's unconscious. Bernie has heard a wife talk about her husband's *apathy* (when she meant to say *empathy*), a boyfriend complain that he "was not turned on when I *killed* her" (meaning when he *kissed* his girlfriend), and a woman cheerfully express that her parents were *never* there for her . . . though she thought she was saying *always*.

As helpful as they can be, Freudian slips actually occur very infrequently, so it's important to understand what they are, identify them when they happen, and to write them down in that journal you're keeping. Like a dream, a Freudian slip is the conscious expression of something suppressed in the unconscious mind. It's a perfectly understandable occurrence, when you think about it: if speaking is a way of expressing what's on your conscious mind, doesn't it make sense that your unconscious mind is going to try to slip in a word or two once in a while?

So on those rare instances when you commit an act of parapraxis (that's the fancy term for "slip of the tongue") in relation to your partner—don't dismiss what you've said as a mistake, but instead see it as an opportunity to understand your *whole* mind. Take a look at what you've said and try to find the meaning behind the slip. Are you really angry in some way you'd rather not deal with? Is there something about your partner that is annoying or upsetting you? Whether it seems innocuous or leaves you completely red-faced, your Freudian slip was made by *you* and it came from the depths of *your* unconscious . . . so the smart, relationship-enhancing reaction to it is this: "What can it tell me about *me?*"

Emotional Overreactions

Though I've never been much of a Trekkie, I have to admit that I hadn't ever thought about the role of emotion in my daily life until I watched an episode of *Star Trek: The Next Generation,* and became intrigued with a strange character named Data. "Data's a robot?" I asked my brother, who—after chiding me for my keen grasp of the obvious—corrected me. "Data's an android," he said. "Aside from the yellow eyes and the metallic-colored skin, he seems like a person in every way. Except he has no feelings." A few episodes later, I got it: Data's tragedy is that he gets to have most normal human experiences, but he never *feels* anything about them. Though he can remember millions of jokes, he never quite "gets" why people laugh at them. He can recognize when self-preservation demands he get away from the bad guys, but he's never *scared* of the Romulans or the Borg. (Boy, for a guy who isn't a Trekkie, I know *way* too much about *Star Trek.*) He can understand, logically, that someone has died, but he can't feel *grief* over the loss of that person.

In one of the movies spun off from *Star Trek: The Next Generation,* Data gets an emotion chip implanted in his android brain, and he goes a little crazy. Seems the chip is too much, and Data can't modulate his newly emotional reactions to things. Stupid jokes send him into uncontrollable fits of laughter, things that you and I might find mildly annoying push Data into a complete rage. In other words, Data starts behaving like a child. Think about it: isn't part of growing up learning to control your emotions? Age brings self-control *and* perspective, and eventually you learn that your emotional responses have to have some correlation to the things to which you're responding. A minor occurrence calls for a minor response (or no response at all), while a major event—like a moment of extreme danger, or the achievement of a lifelong goal—can trigger a strong emotional response. You learn to save your big emotional guns, such as terror and despair, for times when they're called for. With age and experience, your conscious mind learns to dial the strength of your emotional responses up or down as needed.

But before we get to how the unconscious can mess with that dial and cause your emotional responses to become way out of proportion to the situations that trigger them, let's step back and look at a few simple truths about your emotional life. First off, you're emotional. We all are. Human beings have a biological inclination to "feel"—that is, parts of our brain are activated under certain conditions and produce predictable reactions . . . what we call emotional responses. That's why you cry at sad movies, or become anxious when taking a test. Sometimes you experience two emotions at once: say a friend hits the lotto for $20 million, and you find yourself feeling terrifically happy for them *and* wildly jealous at the same time.

The proportionality of an emotion—the relationship between the seriousness of an event in your life and the power of your emotional reaction to it—is as automatic as the emotion itself. Say, for instance, that someone you love dies. You automatically (and naturally) feel a great deal of sadness and grief.

Obviously, you're going to feel a lot *less* grief if the person who has died is instead the distant relative of an acquaintance of yours. If the deceased is someone to whom you have absolutely no connection, you might briefly think that it's sad they're gone, but feel no emotion whatsoever. Emotion is proportional.

Except when it's not.

If the death of that person you have no connection to causes you to become hysterical and inconsolable, that's a good sign that it's time to look inward. An *emotional overreaction* is an emotional response to an event or a person that is completely out of whack with what it should be. It's when an adult runs screaming in terror from a small spider, or when a parent carries on so much about a glass of spilled milk that you'd think the child who accidentally knocked the glass over was an ax murderer. Emotional overreactions, like dreams and Freudian slips, are the unconscious mind's way of sending you information. Unfortunately, they tend to be a very loud way for that information to surface.

A parent who screams violently at his or her child over a minor thing (as in spilled milk) is releasing a lot of stored anger. Repressed, unconscious anger. When the milk hits the tablecloth, the minor anger over the child's carelessness attaches itself to—and triggers—the repressed anger, and you end up with one seriously pissed-off parent. (Not to mention a terrified kid, which is why it's so critical to examine emotional overreactions and deal with whatever is causing them.)

Nowhere is the emotional overreaction more common than in romantic relationships. Which makes a lot of sense, when you consider that a "couple" consists of two unrelated people—that is, two people who don't have the same internalized experiences and therefore don't always know when they're about to push each other's sensitive psychological buttons. When buttons get pushed, emotional overreactions are usually the result.

By way of example, imagine the Smiths, sitting at home on a Saturday afternoon. Bob Smith watches a baseball game on television, while his wife Cathy sits at the kitchen table, going through her e-mail on a laptop. "Honey, would you mind getting me a soda?" Bob calls from the next room. Cathy instantly becomes enraged. "Why don't you get off your butt and get your own soda?" she responds. "It's like you think I'm your servant or something!"

Bob, suddenly furious as well, starts shouting at her from his seat on the couch, accusing her of never doing anything for him and wondering how he ended up with such a shrill, unkind spouse.

That, of course, is the double whammy: both partners having emotional overreactions at the same time. In counseling—which they clearly needed—it was revealed that Cathy grew up in a home where her father constantly demeaned her mother, and so she reacted to her husband's simple (and benign) request as if it were an angry demand. Bob, on the other hand, grew up in a household where his mother constantly criticized his father . . . and Bob grew to resent his father for never fighting back. He reacted to his wife as though she were his criticizing mother.

Without those unconscious triggers, the scene would have played out differently. Bob would have made his request, Cathy would either have done what he asked or begged off, in which case Bob would have gotten his own drink. No big deal. When the "no big deal" situations in your relationship seem to mysteriously *become* big deals, that's a sure sign that one or both of you are experiencing emotional overreactions. The worst thing you can do when those overreactions arise is to ignore them or gloss over them. If you do, it's pretty much guaranteed that they'll come back, over and over—and your conflict with your partner will grow.

Instead, recognize the emotional overreaction (if it's yours) as a sign of something troubling within your own unconscious. Take a step back. Take a breath. Grab your journal. Try to describe, in writing, every aspect of your overreaction. Start with the *type* of exaggerated response you had—too much anger, too much sadness, and so forth—and see if that gives you any clue as to what could be causing it. Then describe the circumstances under which you became so emotional: what triggered your behavior? Usually, you'll be able to identify (and start dealing with) the causes of your emotional overreactions. If you're stymied, though, then you might seriously consider seeking therapy. Left unidentified and untreated, the emotional overreaction can be one of the most severe stumbling blocks to a happy, satisfying relationship.

Repetitive Behavior Patterns

Human beings are nothing if not habitual, and that includes you. Chances are pretty good that you live by some kind of schedule. You tend to eat in the same types of restaurants.

You socialize within a fairly well-defined set of friends. In other words, you act in ways that are predictable and comforting. Like most of us, *you've figured out what works for you, and you're sticking with it.*

It's easy enough to see that the reason for this is that repetitive behavior can take the guesswork out of life. Repetitive behavior—the good kind—is the result of internalized experience: through trial and error, you've found out which behaviors either make you feel good or prompt positive responses from the people around you (or both), and then you repeat those behaviors again and again and again. (I have a friend, Amy, who never calls her mom—or takes her mom's calls—after seven P.M. She explained to me that it's a stress-relieving habit: "I never know if it's been a two-martini night. After two martinis, my mom has way too much to say about my love life.") When a repetitive behavior works for you, there's not a lot of need to question it.

The questions should come when the thing you're consistently doing *isn't* working for you, and yet you're doing it again and again and again anyway. My first obviously negative repetitive behavior pattern started in college. No matter how many times I told myself at the start of each semester that "*this* time I'm going to be on top of my work; this time I'll be better organized and more conscientious," I always seemed to wind up in panic mode by the time midterms came around. All the promises to myself about starting term papers early got broken, all the vows to improve my study habits (and not cram everything into the night before the exam) were forgotten. I *knew* how foolish I was being, and yet I put myself in the same situation semester after semester.

Actually, I'm wrong. That pattern didn't start in college; it's how I spent my entire academic life, from elementary school on up. Though the stakes seemed much higher in college—and the workload was certainly more daunting—I had been a scholastic procrastinator all of my life.

It's easy to dismiss that repetitive behavior pattern as "laziness," but trust me: my life was made much harder by my lousy study habits. On those rare occasions when I did manage to get ahead of my work, I found it easier to do, far less stressful, and much more rewarding in terms of my grade point average and self-esteem. So why on earth couldn't I break out of the self-destructive pattern?

You'd have to ask my unconscious. It's that unconscious, once again, that's behind patterns of behavior we'd like to do away with but can't. (Understood properly, the typical New Year's resolution is an attempt to sic the conscious on the unconscious, as in, "I know this behavior is self-destructive, and I'm going to will myself to stop it." Ninety-nine percent of the time, I wouldn't count on the conscious winning the battle.)

Repetitive behavior patterns are one of the more easily identified ways your unconscious makes itself known . . . to you *and* the people around you. We all have friends who pick lousy romantic partners over and over again, vowing each time a relationship ends that they're going to stop choosing so horribly. After a while,

> Repetitive behavior patterns are one of the more easily identified ways your unconscious makes itself known . . . to you *and* the people around you.

we just start to assume that the new partner they're going to introduce us to at dinner will have every bad trait the last ten partners had. We use our knowledge of our friend's pattern to lower our expectations . . . and as a warning that there's no point in getting attached to our friend's latest flame.

Knowing someone's repetitive behavior pattern certainly has advantages. Early in his career as a therapist, Bernie worked in a clinic where one of his responsibilities was to interview therapists who applied for staff positions. Bernie reviewed résumés and arranged personal interviews. He was constantly amazed at how much could be learned about an applicants' personality—and not just their work history—through a careful reading of their résumé. For example, a fifty-year-old therapist sent a résumé that showed that he'd never been at any one job for more than two years. His references were terrific, and people that he'd worked with in the past seemed to genuinely like him, so Bernie quickly ruled out antisocial behavior as the cause of his professional rootlessness. Partially because the clinic wasn't sure what it's staffing needs would be down the road, Bernie recommended him for the job, betting that the man would stick to his usual pattern. Turns out the guy was a great employee . . . who quit the job almost exactly two years later, just as predicted.

Bernie has found over time that repetitive behavior patterns are excellent predictors of his relationships with individual patients. So much so that he asks the same question of everyone who seeks out his services as a therapist: "What experiences have you had with other therapists?" When someone tells him that they've been in therapy three or four times over the course of their life, but never managed to stay with a therapist for more than three months, he takes it as a pretty solid guarantee that they'll find (or manufacture) a reason to end their sessions with *him* before long. While he used to believe that the therapists preceding him hadn't been up to the task at hand—and *he'd* be the one to finally help his new patient—Bernie has come to learn that his professional ego is no match for an entrenched repetitive behavior pattern.

It's that entrenchment, that long history of a certain pattern of behavior, which makes changing the behavior so difficult. But even if you can't change your own repetitive behaviors, or those of your partner, you can make your relationship stronger by learning to identify them and by understanding their nature. Time to pick up that journal again, and under the heading of "Repetitive Behaviors," write down as many of your more recent resolutions (New Year's and any others) that you can remember. Write down all the things you do repeatedly that you wish you didn't, that cause you stress, or that you simply can't understand. Later on, when we've filled up some of that journal with memories and observations about your upbringing, you'll be able to flip back to this list and see just how rooted its content is in your childhood . . . and *not* in your current relationship.

Like each of the other "exit doors" of the unconscious we've looked at, repetitive behavior patterns are by-products of personality, and therefore can tell you a great deal about the person who possesses them. Especially yourself. So instead of standing around with friends on New Year's Eve, vowing to use willpower to change the behaviors that consistently cause you anxiety, try using brainpower to try to understand what those behaviors are saying about *you*.

Symptoms

One day the discovery was made that the symptoms of disease in certain nervous patients have meaning.

—Sigmund Freud

Really, Dr. Freud? You think? When Freud wrote the above, I suspect it was met by mothers everywhere with a knowing sigh: anyone who's ever had to deal with a nervous child's stomachache on the first day of school knows instinctively the connection between the mind and the body.

Clinically speaking, the term *symptom* means a disease process, something in a functional unit that isn't working. A malfunction, if you will. When we find ourselves faced with medical symptoms, like pain, fever, or lethargy, for example, we get ourselves to the doctor in the hopes that he or she will be able to treat us, and make the symptoms go away. Often, they can do just that. But almost as often—in something like 40 percent of all patient visits—doctors are unable to come up with diagnoses: they can't find any *physical* reason their patients are having symptoms. Which means the origin of those symptoms might well be psychological . . . in other words, an unconscious, physical expression of something the patient hasn't been able to express (or even realize) consciously.

The statistic I just used gives you some idea of how prevalent physically based psychological symptoms are. Add unexplained physical ailments to the more commonly understood signs of psychological distress—such as depression, phobias, and anxiety—and you start to realize why there are so many doctors practicing psychiatry and psychology. The unconscious creates a never-ending patient stream.

Compared to a psychotherapist, of course, the general practitioner usually has it easy. Medical symptoms can point to clear diagnoses, which lead to common treatments. Your fever and aches cause the doctor to take a blood test, a virus is identified, you're given a prescription and sent home to bed . . . and that's pretty much that. (Obviously, many of the symptoms that send people to the doctor are far worse than the ones I've described, and many times there isn't an easy cure— or any cure at all—for what's causing the symptoms, but you get my point: medicine tends to be cut-and-dried.)

A psychological symptom is much harder to treat, because it *always* has its roots in the unconscious. As psychologist Norman Cameron wrote, "There should be no mystery about the unintelligibility of . . . symptoms [because] almost all of the processes entering into symptom formation are themselves unconscious. We see only the end product."

If you look at dreams and Freudian slips as one end of the spectrum, on the other end of the ways your unconscious seeks conscious expression you'll find the psychological symptom. This sign of unconscious trouble is easily the most serious— and certainly the most frightening—and almost always needs some form of treatment, both to identify the origin and to begin to alleviate the anxiety that it's causing you. If something in your unconscious is so upsetting that it brings on physical or psychological pain, it's time to move beyond self-analysis and into . . . well, *analysis.*

Our unconscious breaks through and becomes conscious in five ways:

1. Dreams
2. Freudian Slips
3. Emotional Overreactions
4. Repetitive Behavior Patterns
5. Symptoms

As you might expect, it's those symptoms that almost always drive people into therapists' offices. Whether it's depression or a baffling compulsion, a chronic stomachache (as in the case of Abigail, she of the "relation*shit*"), or a constant anxiety, developing a serious symptom is your mind's way of telling you that it's time to call in a professional.

A psychological symptom usually spells doom for a relationship when it's left untreated, for a pretty obvious reason: we're all frightened of the unknown. When a partner starts showing a psychological symptom, and then protests that he or she has no idea where it's coming from, it's natural to start imagining the worst. (Your partner must not want to tell you what's upsetting him . . . so it must be you!) If you think about it, that's why the silent treatment is so effective in wounding someone you're upset with: in the absence of information, the mind has a way of jumping to the worst possible conclusion and adding to your misery. Clearly, it's critical to seek help when the unconscious mind is wreaking havoc with your life.

No matter what path your unconscious has chosen in its quest to get your attention, it's always critical to recognize the information that it's revealing to you. And to collect that information in one place—this is why I'm being a noodge about your journal—so that you can start to see patterns. The principle is the same whether you're experiencing something as benign as a confusing dream or as malignant as a panic attack: the more information you can gather on the aspects of your personality that are causing you fear, anxiety, or actual physical pain, the better equipped you'll be to manage your distress . . . *and* your partner's.

3

Chemistry Lessons

My high-school science teacher used to start each class with a review. Sounds counterintuitive, I know, but what I learned from her class was that the best way to get yourself focused on what you're about to learn is through a minireview of where you've recently been. So in her honor, I'll steal the line with which she started every class: "Now, where were we?"

Here's where we've been:

- You are born with physical *and* psychological needs.
- It's the degree to which your parents and caregivers were able to satisfy those psychological needs that determines how gratifying (or not) your interpersonal world will be . . . that is, how successful you'll

be at forming relationships as an adult that are positive and productive.

- Your personality, though it contains some genetic predispositions, is mostly shaped by the experiences you internalized.

- Your personality has unconscious elements, which figure prominently in the romantic choices you make . . . and in the ultimate course of all of your romantic relationships.

- Through learning to interpret the signals your unconscious sends you all the time, you can better understand not only your romantic choices, but also why you have the conflicts that you do within those romantic relationships.

And finally,

- That John Travolta–Bruce Willis movie about the talking baby is incredibly misleading.

Okay, we haven't really covered that last thing. I just wanted to see if you were paying attention. But since I raised the issue, have you ever seen the movie *Look Who's Talking*? In it, single guy John Travolta finds himself surrogate parenting an infant whose every thought is heard by the audience, in the voice of Bruce Willis. We see the cute little kid on the screen while in voice-over we hear his (largely sarcastic) take on what's happening around him. The movie was very successful, but also very misleading: if a newborn could talk, he wouldn't waste his time with sitcom wisecracks. No, he'd probably look mom or dad in the eye, and say something like this:

"Now, listen up: I need you to feel good about me. I need you to feel warm, loving, caring, protective, and nurturing. I don't have time for *your* problems, so keep your depressions, anxieties, and marital problems out of my nursery here. Nothing should interfere with the chronically good feelings I need you to show toward me.

"Okay, I'm not *totally* unreasonable, and I guess I understand that there will be things in your life that will bring you down, so if you have occasional bad feelings, I can probably manage it. If you want to get technical about this, what I'm saying is that I can sustain your (infrequent!) bad patches as long as they're within the context of a steady flow of good feeling states. We're bonding here, and as long as the predominant feelings I get from you are good . . . then we're okay.

"If you do your work correctly, I'll be a happy, well-adjusted, thriving infant who eats well, sleeps well, has very little anxiety about strangers, and generally makes you actually feel those good feelings I demand from you.

"I should warn you, it may be that I have a genetic predisposition to be a pain in the neck. That is, I may be the kind of baby who cries a lot or barely sleeps, who has gas or colic. It may be hard for you, at times, to feel good about me, but *you're the adult and I'm the infant,* so you better just deal with anything I throw at you. Don't blame me, don't project your problems on me, and don't ignore or reject me either. Any questions?"

I guess if Bruce Willis had said all that, it wouldn't have been much of a movie. Maybe the wisecracks were a good idea, after all. The thing is, the needs of a newborn are a tall order for just about any parent. Dealing with those needs can be easier or harder depending on how the parent was parented; in fact, the biggest single factor that contributes to the success (or failure) of a parent is the example that parent received when he or she was on the other end of the relationship. It's a circle game, indeed.

> The biggest single factor that contributes to the success (or failure) of a parent is the example that parent received when he or she was on the other end of the relationship.

What our loquacious baby was describing, of course, is the first stage of the relationship between parent and child: the symbiotic stage. This can last through the first six months or so of a child's life. During the symbiotic stage, a child presumably gets all the good feelings she needs and consequently grows and thrives physically and emotionally. At the end of this stage, she'll start trying things such as sitting up or rolling over, and may even learn to crawl. She'll start making her first attempts at communication.

After this stage, a child will start to attempt to separate physically and emotionally from the parent. She'll want to move about a little, explore her world. Her attention is now expanding to take in some of the stuff that exists outside her safe little symbiosis with her parent. If she could manage it, her speech to that parent would now go something like this:

"Hey, thanks for all the good feelings. (And keep 'em coming.) In fact, you've done such a good job of providing gratification that I'm a little more secure, and I'm ready to start seeing who *I* am, independent of you. Let's not go crazy—I'm not moving out or anything—but I need you to hold me a little less and fade into the background a little more. As I take the first few steps toward becoming my own person, your role is now more of a caretaker gig: let me go, watch over me from a little bit of a distance, and be there when I turn around, looking for reassurance. Oh, and strained peas are *disgusting*."

What we see in these early stages of the parent-child relationship is the creation of an attachment, and then the slow disengagement that marks the beginning of a child's physical and psychological independence. If the relationship is emotionally gratifying for the child—if he or she feels secure, loved, and cared for—then the child can *re*-engage with the parent. The child has felt love, so the child learns to return love. The child has been treated with concern and respect, and so the child learns to treat others with concern and respect.

In other words, each of us starts the process of the internalization of experience in the context of an interpersonal relationship—the one with our parent or caregiver—from the earliest days of our life. And that first relationship is remarkably complex, when you stop to think about it. A baby, by virtue of his genetic predisposition, engages his mother in very specific ways; he'll smile, cry, stare, and attempt to cuddle close (or wriggle free). How his mother will react to each of these things is based on a number of factors, including how she was parented, her own personality, how she feels about kids, her mood, and so on. Mother and child influence each other in very powerful ways. Each can produce intense emotional reactions in the other.

Think of the bonding stage, then, as a kind of psychological umbilical cord, which permits mother and child to see directly into the emotional and cognitive states of the other. Each can sense how the other is feeling and how the other "sees" things. Such an intense connection is a double-edged sword: not only can a parent and child have intense feelings of love for each other, but also powerful feelings of anger and frustration . . . and as the father of adolescent girls I can attest that this stage *never* seems to end. Just about every emotion is heightened by the bond between a parent and a child.

But while the intensity of emotions may be similar on both ends of the relationship, the responsibility for the course of the relationship is more one-sided, especially in the earliest days. It is the parent's responsibility to moderate responses to strong emotions. It's the parent's role to maintain the effort—no matter how impossible it might seem at times—to sustain the loving, emotionally gratifying parent-child bond. The parent's emotions, words, attitudes, and ability to relate are all felt by the child through that psychological umbilical cord long before the child can speak, and all of those things have a profound impact on what will become the child's personality.

As an infant starts to internalize the experiences provided by his mother, what he's really doing is internalizing snapshots of the many different relationships he has with her: "Me and Mommy when Mommy is happy," "Me and Mommy when Mommy is angry," "Me and Mommy when Mommy is distant," "Me and Mommy when Mommy is sad," and so on. Think of each of these relationship portraits that the child is taking in as a unit. If there are far more units where Mommy is happy and nurturing, then "Mommy is happy and nurturing" becomes the predominant characteristic of the infant's relationship with the mother. The stronger the characteristic— the more units of "happy Mommy" the baby experiences, for example—the more likely that characteristic will become an enduring part of the child's developing personality.

(And yes, the other people in a baby's life—his father, siblings, babysitters and the like—also add units, depending on their proximity to the child. But because mothers tend to be the primary caregivers, there are typically more "Me and Mommy" units in that budding personality, followed by "Me and Daddy." Close friendships tend to come into the child's life a little late in the game to contribute many units, because by early adolescence the template for his personality is pretty well-set.)

Since all adults have some degree of weakness in their personalities, it makes sense that at least some of the stuff that's transmitted to a child is negative or bad. That's when it's time for the unconscious to step in. It's the unconscious part of the growing personality that internalizes bad traits and then suppresses the memory of that internalization: we remember the stuff that made us kind and loving, but we're not really sure why we're so anxious or short-tempered.

Now, let's take a break from the kids, and talk about *you*.

As your life progressed, you developed a personality structure. You added traits to it both consciously and unconsciously. When it came time to enter into "adult" relationships, you found yourself relating to these new people in ways that you learned from your earliest days . . . those happy, sad, and so on units that you picked up along the way become reactivated with each new relationship. Because the collection of relationships and experiences that created your personality is unlike anyone else's, you are indeed unique; however, you have enough common experiences with the rest of the human race that you can recognize the basic similarities that your thoughts and feelings have with those of other people in your life. For instance, we all get angry; it's just that we do it in different ways, to different degrees, and for different reasons.

So you've got this personality, much of which you're aware of and some of which you aren't, and while it's unique, there are ways in which it will indeed mesh with someone else's personality. There are ways in which your personality feeds off that of others, just as their personalities will feed off of yours. Welcome to the romantic relationship. Welcome to Chemistry 101.

When you meet someone that you find attractive, and begin interacting with them, the initial rush of euphoria you might feel is often chalked up to "chemistry." There's just something that connects us, you think. Your friends (hopefully) say, "You two seem made for each other." Think about that in light of what we've looked at: you really *do* connect— at least at first—when you start off on a romance, because the complementary parts of your personalities are the first ones that are activated during your time together. As you become more emotionally involved, you start to relate to your new love in the internalized ways that you learned from your earliest interpersonal relationships with your family members.

Often you'll find that your conscious needs and desires tend to match those of the person you're involved with. That's the good stuff.

In long-term relationships that are mostly happy and gratifying, the good stuff predominates. Eventually, though, it's possible that the same friends who were so happy about your new relationship become troubled. Maybe they come to you and say, "You seem so different when you're with him." And chances are good that they're right: as your new relationship becomes more involved and committed, there is a greater activation of the unconscious thoughts, feelings, fantasies, attitudes, and expectations that derive from your family. So to your friends, you *seem* different, but it's still you, they just haven't seen these aspects of your personality before. Since we know that the unconscious parts of your personality are the more troubling, their activation doesn't just spook your friends, it often also means the end of the infatuation stage of a relationship.

> When your romantic relationship progresses . . . you'll inevitably notice that the wonderful, euphoric, and optimistic feelings you have toward your partner become intertwined with conflict and complaint.

When your romantic relationship progresses to cohabitation, or to engagement and marriage, you'll inevitably notice that the wonderful, euphoric, and optimistic feelings you have toward your partner become intertwined with conflict and complaint. Mostly, this is a manageable phenomenon: *every* couple has problems, and most couples learn to deal with them.

I know, I just wrote "most couples," and you immediately thought, "No . . . not *most:* there's a 50 percent divorce rate these days, so at best I have a fifty-fifty chance of having my marriage work!" Well, relax a little. Like so many statistics, the oft-quoted 50 percent divorce rate in America is misleading. Here's why: when a conflicted relationship ends in divorce, it's not uncommon for one or both spouses to have someone else waiting in the wings. The conscious fantasy that they're having is that the new relationship will be better and more gratifying than the current dysfunctional one. They're essentially running from one relationship to the next—without wondering what it is within themselves that contributed to the divorce—and they often end up marrying the new person. But it's a pretty safe bet that they've just attached themselves to a person with the same personality characteristics that, when joined to their own, will produce the same problems they've just walked away from. The reason that 50 percent rate is so misleading is that it includes people who have divorced more than once . . . and the divorce rate for *second* marriages is much, much higher.

I bring this up mostly to make the point that Bernie isn't kidding when he talks about patterns of behavior that grow out of the personality we formed in our earliest years, patterns that are predictable, have unconscious elements, and can seem to fly in the face of our own self-interest.

Let's look at the case of Bob Anders, a long-term patient of Bernie's. Bob displayed a textbook case of self-absorption: he needed everyone in his world to admire and adore him, and to make note of his every success. As you might guess, Bob was this way because unconsciously, he felt pretty much the opposite. He secretly felt inadequate and self-critical. As a very young man, he met and married Jessica. While he wasn't very attracted to her, she came from a good family with lots of money, and he sought to better his social standing through their marriage. Years later, Jessica dumped him—big shock, I know—and accused him of chronic criticism and verbal abuse.

Soon after, while he was still a young man, he met and fell in love with a woman named Joan, who in short order became the second Mrs. Anders. Joan consciously felt inferior, inadequate, worthless, stupid—just about every bad thing she could feel about herself—and wondered how someone like Bob could love her. When her new husband treated her with the same callous disregard that he'd shown toward his first wife, Joan accepted the treatment. Yes, she fought back and defended herself, and her marriage was not by any stretch a happy one, but Joan never seriously considered leaving Bob. She never thought anyone else would have her.

The story of how Bob and the two Mrs. Anders got to their sad places in life came out slowly in therapy. Bob, it turns out, was raised by a mother who constantly criticized both Bob and his father. In order to protect himself from the pain of his mother's attacks, Bob developed the fantasy that he was, on the contrary, just about perfect. His mother's statements didn't fit with his self-imposed worldview, so they went through the process of unconscious internalization; that is, no matter how perfect he claimed to be, he secretly felt defective. His personality developed within it two distinct (and opposing) traits: "See, world? I'm perfect! And if I say this loud and long enough, you won't see that I'm really a fraud!"

Add to that duality another bit of repression: Bob hated his mother—can you blame him?—and had to push into his unconscious his desire to attack her.

As he grew and matured, his defensive need to appear perfect became the predominant part of his personality. He became pompous and boastful; he was the bore at the party who has to make sure everyone in the room knows what a good job he has and what kind of car he drives. That "I'm defective" part of his personality got pushed deeper into his unconscious . . . but it would not be ignored. Bob learned to take his feelings of inadequacy and project them onto women. Projection, by the way, is the process by which we unconsciously take the bad feelings we have toward ourselves and attribute them to those around us. When Bob projected his dark side onto the first Mrs. Anders, Jessica, she wouldn't take it from him because her self-image was essentially positive; she didn't recognize in herself the inadequacy he was trying to pin on her. Since he wouldn't stop denigrating her, she walked.

In poor Joan's case, however, the lousy stuff Bob projected matched up very well with her own unconscious feelings about herself. When he attacked her verbally, she fought back mildly—no one likes hearing that they're worthless—but secretly she believed he was right. Even her feeble self-defense enraged him; he wasn't getting any relief from his own unconscious self-loathing if she wouldn't accept it as her own. Which meant Bob got nastier . . . and Joan backed off, because she was terrified that if he rejected her, no one would want her. Each time she backed down, they went through a short period of equilibrium, because each had gotten what they wanted: Bob was able to project his bad thoughts about himself onto someone who would accept them, and Joan had staved off rejection. The ongoing conflict became their basic mode of relating to each other.

Have you ever known a couple that fights so much, and so often, that you cannot for the life of you imagine why they're still together? Well, sometimes, the fights *are* the reason they stay together. In his first marriage, Bob didn't have a receptacle for his projected self-loathing; Jessica wouldn't give him what his unconscious clearly needed. The marriage ended. But in Joan, Bob found someone who enabled him to nurture his own conscious feelings of perfection and omnipotence by accepting his (far darker) unconscious feelings as her own. For all her mild protestations, Joan stayed in the marriage because she found someone who confirmed all her worst thoughts about herself . . . but stuck around, just the same. On some level, each of them wanted the other to be the admiring parent they'd never known; unfortunately, neither of them had much ability for nurturing or compassion. Since they couldn't get from each other the qualities that might have helped them break away from their unconscious self-criticism, they were doomed to repeat their respective childhoods for the entire course of their marriage.

> Have you ever known a couple that fights so much, and so often, that you cannot for the life of you imagine why they're still together? Well, sometimes, the fights *are* the reason they stay together.

Or at least until they spent some quality time on Bernie's couch. After years of marital therapy, Bob and Joan learned to recognize their own insecurities, and to treat each other far more kindly. When each learned what the other was really experiencing, compassion and understanding began to replace constant battling as the normal state of their relationship.

Actually, Bob and the two Mrs. Anders serve as perfect examples of two common psychological processes. With Mrs. Anders the first, Bob practiced *projection,* the process by which we take some unacceptable part of ourselves and randomly put it on someone else. Jessica didn't feel inadequate consciously *or* unconsciously, but Bob kept telling her that she was. With Mrs. Anders the second, Bob moved beyond projection into something known as *projective identification.* By way of explaining the latter, let's dig into an old newspaper story that bore the following headline:

PSYCHIATRIST TESTS, KILLS SLAY SUSPECT

Sounds like something out of one of those fifty-eight spin-offs of *Law & Order,* I know, but it's true: a court-appointed psychiatrist, Manuel Poggi, spent four days giving a suspected murderer named Diaz a battery of tests, and then took his own belt and strangled Diaz, who didn't resist. "I had to do it for the good of society," Poggi said at a news conference held in the police precinct where he'd committed the crime. "The hour had come to apply justice," he said. Poggi told reporters that he'd been driven by frustration into killing Diaz, suspected in eight grisly murders, whom he described as "a monster of superior intelligence." Ironically, there were police guards right outside the room where Poggi and Diaz were talking, put there by the head of the police homicide division, for Poggi's protection. The fact that Diaz didn't call out or try to make some noise that would alert the guards convinced at least one police official that Diaz had actually induced Poggi to murder him. In other words, the official believed that Diaz had committed suicide-by-psychiatrist.

Bernie followed the Poggi story in his local newspaper. A few years later, a remarkably similar story ran:

SUICIDE COUNSELOR CHARGED IN MURDER TRY

This time, a guy working a suicide hotline in California was arrested after admitting to slitting the wrists of a chronic caller. You read me right: the man who was supposed to be talking the depressed caller out of his suicidal feelings actually drove to the caller's house and tried to do him in. His rationale, when caught by the police? The caller "was sucking everything out of me . . . he antagonized me so that I would kill him."

According to Bernie, the story is as explainable as it is astonishing. The suicidal caller was unconsciously filled with rage, which he dealt with by turning it inward and transforming it into severe depression . . . suicidal depression. Unaware of his own rage, he started calling the suicide hotline and became almost completely dependent on the volunteer who answered his calls. Over the course of several conversations, the caller induced what became a murderous rage in the volunteer, a rage so powerful that the volunteer had to vent it by . . . trying to kill the caller. It's important to note that the caller couldn't have elicited that reaction out of just anybody—we're not all simply waiting for the right person to release our inner Hannibal Lecter—and in fact he had unconsciously selected a volunteer who had murderous rage as a component of his own personality. Had you or I taken the suicidal man's calls, chances are good we'd have found some other (less homicidal) way to vent the rage he projected into us.

Obviously, these are extreme examples. Both Diaz and the suicide hotline caller were deeply disturbed men who were able to induce deeply disturbing feeling states into the people they had access to. Both used the process of projective identification in an effort to achieve an aim that . . . well, would qualify them for episodes on one of those fifty-eight *Law & Order* spin-offs. Most folks, though, use the process a little differently.

When we talk about *projection,* we're talking about the process of putting some undesirable part of ourselves *onto* someone else; *projective identification,* then, is the process of taking that undesirable part and putting it *into* someone else. What we are really doing is making that other person feel or experience what we're trying to exorcise. Here's where most of us part company with Diaz and the suicide hotline caller: once we've projected our unwanted stuff into someone else, we want to keep that other person close at hand, so we can continuously feel relief. In other words, as long as they feel the horrible stuff we've put into them, we don't have to.

That's not an easy distinction to understand, so let's stay with it a moment, and consider the fundamental difference between projection and projective identification. Projection is the quick fix, where we randomly ascribe something we hate about ourselves to just about anyone else: our partner, the guy living down the street, the woman on television. Then we reject that person, and by doing so we reject the aspect of ourselves that we're trying to shake off. The problem is, projection never works for very long, because the thing we're trying to rid ourselves of never actually goes anywhere. It will continue to make itself known to us, and we'll have to project it onto others again and again. Projective identification, on the other hand, is an attempt at a long-term solution to our self-loathing, because *we keep the receptacle of our lousy feelings close at hand, so we can* constantly *delude ourselves that we're really okay.* (That alone probably explains a lot of your friends' marriages to you.)

There's one other component of projective identification that makes it so suitable for married couples: unlike the act of projection, which can be done randomly, to practice projective identification, you have to choose your target carefully. You have to choose someone who has a part of his personality that's very much like the part of yours you want to get rid of. Most often, that choice is unconscious: it's not like you wake up one morning and say, "Today I've gotta find me a guy with inadequacy issues, so I can feel superior, for once." Instead, you'll sense the other person's personality defect on a level you're not aware of . . . and though you think it's his dashing smile and quick wit, it's actually your unconscious recognition of that defect that makes him attractive to you. Some of the longest lasting marriages begin when two people find in each other someone with whom they can projectively identify.

Take the Bensons, for example. When they came to Bernie, Samantha Benson was a forty-year-old woman who had experienced several periods of psychiatric hospitalization. She had been diagnosed with paranoid schizophrenia, a disorder whose symptoms can include hallucinations (seeing things that aren't there) and delusions (believing things that aren't true). Her husband of twenty years, Paul, seemed to be quite the opposite of his wife: he came across as well-adjusted, happy, calm . . . in other words, he seemed perfectly mentally healthy.

Early on in their sessions, Bernie sussed out a pattern to her hospitalizations: when Paul experienced any degree of anxiety or stress, he would attack his wife verbally, calling her "crazy" and threatening to leave her. Samantha would become symptomatic—that is, she'd start seeing things and having delusions—and would have to be hospitalized. Her absence would allow Paul to calm down. He'd become conciliatory and nurturing, and (when she would inevitably be released from the psych ward) the relationship would go back to a period of stability.

A little backstory might help here. Paul came from a family of highly disturbed people. His brother and both of his sisters were schizophrenic, and required constant care, which as a dutiful sibling, he gave. Home life took its toll on Paul, though, because he developed an unconscious anxiety that one day he, too, could become schizophrenic. Samantha did indeed have a history of mental illness, which Paul knew when he fell in love with and married her.

You can write the script, I'm sure. Paul fell in love with Samantha partially because of the unconscious recognition that he could maintain his own sanity by keeping someone with actual mental illness close. When his anxieties bubbled up during times of stress, he could practice a little projective identification; he could discharge his anxiety by accusing his wife of the very thing he was afraid of for himself, and be so successful in his badgering that she would actually manifest the symptoms. (How many times do we yell at a partner, in exasperation, "You're driving me crazy!" For Paul and Samantha, that cliché was the literal truth.)

In the Benson marriage, like in most marriages, projective identification was a two-way street. Samantha's version was a great deal more positive, however. In Paul, she found someone who was—when not in a state of anxiety—a very nurturing man; he'd cared physically and emotionally for three schizophrenic siblings. Her bouts of mental illness brought out the caretaker in Paul: she induced in him the positive and warm feelings that were locked in her unconscious because she'd never experienced them within her own family, growing up.

I saw a gag gift at a store not long ago, a little black cotton onesie meant for a newborn. Printed on the front, in thin white letters, was, "It's not me. It's you." And you know what? That's a remarkably astute joke: from our earliest days, we are projective identifiers. As newborns, we induce feelings in our mother, just as she induces them in us. Our mother then reacts to the feelings we've induced in her, and then hopefully reacts to us in a way that promotes positive growth and psychological development in us. That bond with our mother is the first interpersonal relationship we'll ever have, and it becomes the basis for the way we see the world, and the way we carry on future relationships.

Every infant is born with the capacity to experience (and express) a variety of powerful emotional states, such as anger, pleasure, anxiety, fatigue, and the like. The infant feels each of these things intensely, and doesn't have any way to reduce, moderate, or modify any of the feelings that she experiences. So she cries, or doesn't eat, or becomes restless, or does any one of the thousand things that babies do in an unconscious attempt to communicate. I use the word *unconscious* here because a baby doesn't understand her own stress . . . she just knows she's miserable. (Come to think of it, those unconscious methods of communicating unhappiness never really leave us, not even after we've learned to use words, and deal with most of our needs ourselves. I *still* don't eat when I'm really upset . . . only now, my mom doesn't come along and make it all better.)

When a baby communicates distress, her parents almost literally feel her pain. Thanks to the almost psychic bond created by the constant flow of induced feelings, mothers and fathers react intensely to the signals being given by their children. Ask any parent and they'll tell you: when someone else's kid cries, they barely register it. When their own baby starts to wail, they'd just about give up their eyeteeth to make the crying stop. It's the job of the mother or father to experience the infant's distress and to figure out a way to reduce it. At the same time, the parent has to try to contain the emotional state, and respond to the child's distress in a calm, caring, and concerned way, which can be a pretty tall order when a child has been up all night, or has been fussy for hours.

Projective identification is the first and most primitive form of communication; it's the first way infants learn to communicate with their parents. Think of the bond created through projective identification as a feedback loop, where feelings (either good or bad) constantly bounce back and forth from parent to child and from child to parent. When an infant is relaxed, he'll coo and smile and snuggle and thereby induce warm, loving, and nurturing feelings in his mother. Those feelings are returned in the smiles, soft words, and obvious happiness the infant receives from her. When a child is not so happy, things go differently. A negative feedback loop seems to come equipped with an amplifier: the baby, in his distress, cries and carries on so that his mother will serve as a tension-reducer . . . a role that becomes exponentially harder for her, considering all the tension the baby is causing. She's supposed to contain the unpleasant feelings put in her by her baby, by using her rational, understanding self along with her psychological defense mechanisms to reduce the intensity of those feelings. When she's able to reduce the power of those induced feelings, she feels less distress, and signals the baby to feel less distress.

Which is a heck of a lot harder than returning coos and smiles. Being the tension-reducer requires a great deal of effort. And sometimes, Mom just isn't up to the task.

In all of this projecting and re-projecting of powerful emotional states, sometimes there's a breakdown, and the mother cannot serve the stress reduction role that her baby needs her to. Maybe she's immature or has plenty of stress of her own. Maybe she has psychological problems that keep her from being able to reduce the intensity of the feelings her child is projecting into her. If any of those are the case, then the mother might very well amplify the baby's distress and re-project it. The feedback loop between mother and baby means that the distress level doesn't fall, and the relationship becomes characterized by painful, negative feelings. Which isn't good for either of them, but can be especially harmful to the baby.

Again, think of projective identification as the first communication between parent and child, one that doesn't involve language but rather the mutual induction of emotional states in each other. If these internal states seem strong to the mother, just imagine how they affect the child, who has no other psychological framework to compare them to. Everything the child knows, she has learned through the bond with her mother. The regular presence of positive emotional states— like love, comfort, and caring—makes it not only easier for the child to form solid, caring relationships with others later on, but it also helps the child develop physically and emotionally. If the vast majority of feelings shared between mother and child are negative—such as anxiety, anger, tension, and physical distress—it's far harder for a child to mature in just about every way. (Though it is easier for her to eventually get a book deal, if her mom is Joan Crawford.)

There's a little bit of the old chicken-and-the-egg thing going on here, because a child is both the recipient of the feeling states from his parents and the creator of those states. How his parents respond to him is determined in large part by how they experience him—is he an easy baby? a difficult baby? were they emotionally ready to be parents?—and he in turn begins to internalize their responses to him. The child who receives mostly warm, loving feelings internalizes those states and grows up to feel secure, worthy, loved, and desirable. He becomes the kid with plenty of self-esteem and a healthy sense of who he is. But in those early days he's not only taking in the feeling states, he's also forming a mental picture of the relationship through which those states are being conveyed: "Me and Mommy" becomes a rough psychological blueprint for later relationships. (Typically, "me and Mommy" is the blueprint that infants of both genders will unconsciously use in seeking out romantic partners, and also for developing self-esteem. The child's idea of "me and Daddy" also has a strong impact on issues of self-esteem, but most often figures into later love relationships a bit less than "me and Mommy.")

The very core of self-esteem is determined and shaped by the relationship between a developing child and the parent with whom he or she is primarily bonded with, which is why I've used the word *mommy* so much in this chapter. As a child matures, the other parent comes into focus for him, as do any siblings, caretakers, or extended family members. Each of these folks contributes to (and can modify) the child's growing self-image. Each of these folks becomes another mental picture of another relationship with the child: in time, he'll add "Sister and me" and "Nana and me" to his expanding repertoire. Eventually, he'll start internalizing the relationships between the people he knows, such as "Mommy and Daddy." All of these primary relationships serve as the building blocks of every area of personality development, self-image, and, ultimately, will determine with whom the child will one day fall in love.

Here's a (romantic) chemistry lesson: when we're actively seeking romantic relationships as adults, we start projecting all over again. We project our internal world—all those "me and Mommy," "me and Daddy," "Mommy and Daddy" relationships we've been carrying around in our developed personalities—onto potential mates, and in effect we re-create both the best and worst of our past experiences. It's really kind of remarkable how much we will ultimately treat people in exactly the ways in which we were treated, both positively and negatively. (Okay, maybe it's not so remarkable: what else would we know how to do, but to recycle our own experiences? I have a brother who, when he's unhappy, projects the worst of his "me and Daddy" stuff onto everyone in his path. When he does it to me, I'm always torn between being pissed at him and being really impressed by how precisely he's able to channel our pop.)

We perceive people as attractive and desirable once we unconsciously recognize that they contain within them psychological elements that will help us re-create our past relationships . . . again, both the positive and negative ones. We tend to develop love relationships based on the other person's capacity to re-create certain feeling states within us, and relationship patterns that we're unconsciously comfortable with. So if our earliest days consisted of positive projective identification, we'll choose people based on our wish to give, nurture, love, protect, and cherish. But if that childhood of ours was marked by mostly negative feeling states being passed back and forth between us and one or both parents, we'll go on seeking those lousy feeling states all over again.

Once we've found the person we're looking for, we start inducing whatever feelings *we* have in *them*. If we're sending them the good stuff, we tend to get good stuff in return, and chances are good we'll have a gratifying relationship where we love each other and manage to handle the normal conflicts and disagreements of a relationship just fine. If our feelings are mostly negative though, we'll project that, and be on our way to a conflicted relationship where our partner returns our anger and anxiety in a feedback loop of misery.

> If that childhood of ours was marked by mostly negative feeling states being passed back and forth between us and one or both parents, we'll go on seeking those lousy feeling states all over again.

Which begins to explain my friend Lisa, the smart, beautiful girl I met in college who eventually married an abusive, self-centered jerk. It won't surprise you that he was merely the last in a long string of what she called "bad boys," men who varied in their physical looks, but who shared two common traits. None of them were particularly successful, academically or in terms of their careers, and all of them—following an initial bout of sweet talk—ultimately spoke to Lisa as if she were an idiot. Actually, they all shared a third trait, as well: when they weren't talking down to Lisa, they weren't talking to her at all. Through each boyfriend, and ultimately through her husband, Lisa re-created both of her parental relationships, which I realized years later after spending time with her family and asking about her childhood. Lisa's dad, completely caught up in his career and his overwhelming narcissism, had largely ignored his daughter; one night she told me (after several shots of that truth serum known as tequila) that her mother once admitted Lisa was unplanned . . . and hinted that she was unwanted as well.

Lisa's mom didn't just tell her daughter horrible things however. She criticized her as well. Unceasingly. From her earliest days, Lisa could remember having every accomplishment belittled, every moment of self-satisfaction derided. After coming home with a second-place trophy won after an eight-team weekend field hockey tournament held in another state, Lisa's mom greeted her with, "You went that far to *lose?*" And though she could rationally see her accomplishments, her brains, and her beauty, Lisa unconsciously felt like a loser.

But here's the important part of the story, in terms of understanding the process of projective identification: Lisa had not only internalized her torment, she had also internalized her tormentors. That is, there was an unconscious part of Lisa's personality that was bullying, just as there was a part that was dismissive. So her romantic relationships became semicomplicated bouts of projectively identifying. Let's review the process by looking at Lisa's situation:

1. Lisa wanted to "cast out" of herself the unacceptable and discomforting parts of her personality.

2. In choosing romantic partners—and ultimately a husband—Lisa *un*consciously sought out men who had within their personalities the exact same traits she consciously thought she was trying to exorcise. In this case, she found men who were not terribly successful (and shared her secret feelings of inadequacy) and who were by turns critical (like her mother) and chilly (like her father).

3. Lisa induced her unacceptable feeling states in her partners; she got them to feel her own pain and then project it back into her.

4. By maintaining these ongoing relationships, she maintained her own equilibrium psychologically: she alternately experienced and rejected her most negative feelings.

Through negative projective identification, your partner comes to represent the unacceptable parts of yourself. (If there aren't any particularly unacceptable parts of your personality—if your early years were characterized by positive feelings—then you tend to project good things *into* the people in your life, not bad things.) Because projective identification is the earliest mode of communication between parent and child, it is the force through which the bedrock of your personality was formed, and also the source of your self-esteem. It's also the source of that chemistry you feel with a new romantic partner.

So now that we've gotten a handle on why you've chosen that person you're romantically involved with, let's take a look at how a love relationship works.

Or doesn't, as the case may be.

Master the Awesome Power of the P. I.

Sorry, couldn't help myself. Just having a little fun with all the 3,867 self-help books that have the words *unleash, secret, master,* and/or *inner* in the title. (*Master the Secrets of Unleashing Your Inner . . .* you get the picture.) Ever notice that those books always seem to be written by guys with huge, frightening smiles; guys who, armed with little more than repackaged common sense, make millions running seminars and selling motivational CDs?

I'd like to humbly offer my own little bit of common sense, something I suspect you'd have come to yourself once the concept of projective identification had some time to marinate in your head a little: with some minor effort, you can use P. I. to help a distressed partner. (Unless you're the cause of their distress. In that case, you're going to have to get a bit farther into this book before you can start to help them.)

Here's the PVM Three-Steps-to-Mastering-Awesome-Equilibrium Plan™—is my smile frightening yet?—that can help you elevate your partner's mood . . . and thereby protect your own.

Step One: **Disengage.** Whatever the cause of your partner's stress—and whatever obnoxious things your partner is doing to let you know just how stressed he or she is—don't take any of it personally. Deal with them the way an animal trainer might: ignore the behavior you don't like, and reward the stuff you do. (Amy Sutherland got a whole book out of the use of animal training techniques in the real world, called *Kicked, Bitten, and Scratched*. Man, I wish I'd had that book growing up.)

The point of disengaging is to keep from being dragged down. What a miserable partner usually does is a form of projective identification: they make you feel lousy so they have some company. Don't join them. If you need to, put some physical space between you, so that you can get to our next step.

Step Two: **Self-Elevate.** I saw a movie not long ago where one of the characters, in a moment of terror, shuts his eyes tight, sticks his fingers in his ears, and starts chanting, "I'm in my happy place! I'm in my happy place!" Good joke, and good advice: to elevate your mood, think of things that make you happy. Shut the rest of the world (including that unhappy partner) out for a bit, and concentrate on thoughts or memories that can reliably bring you some joy. Take some deep breaths while you do this; calm your body along with your mind. Ready?

Step Three: **Radiate.** It's time to beat your miserable partner at their own involuntary game. Instead of letting *them* project their unhappiness into you, you're going to project the calm, happy state you've achieved on your own into *them*. If you find yourself slipping, if their mood is too much for yours, then repeat the steps: disengage, self-elevate, and radiate. You know how a partner's mood can wear you down? Don't let it. Wear theirs *up*, instead.

4.

The Life Cycle of the Relationship

Happily ever after.

There, we're finished. You can turn the page now. I mean, you're reading this chapter to understand what happens after we find a partner, right? And you've seen a million movies, yes? So what can Bernie and I tell you that you don't already know? *Happily ever after.*

Still here? Good. Because that means you've figured out what's wrong with most of the love stories

> "Happily ever after" is a big old cop-out.

you've seen on both the big and the small screen: they end just as the relationships depicted in them actually begin. "Happily ever after" is a big old cop-out.

Take *Pretty Woman,* one of the most popular romantic movies of the last two decades. In it, girl-from-the-wrong-side-of-the-tracks Julia Roberts falls for business tycoon Richard Gere. He shows her what it's like to have a lavish lifestyle, she teaches him to push away from the conference table once in a while and enjoy life. She discovers opera, he discovers the joys of fixing the companies he buys, and not selling them for parts. Just as they seem to be heading toward a relationship, there's a little crisis—did I mention that she's a hooker? or that his lawyer wants to bed her?—and they split up. Until he comes to his senses, of course, and overcomes his fear of heights to climb the fire escape of her building, the better to prove his love.

The end. In fact, the movie really *is* meant as a fairy tale—albeit one with streetwalkers—and the way you know that is in the last exchange between Gere and Roberts. He asks what a princess does when a prince rescues her, and she responds, "She rescues him right back." Cue Roberts's megawatt smile, and roll credits. I remember a mildly cynical moment after I left the theater that night when I explained to my wife that they had to end the movie there, because how could they ever survive as a couple, once the gossip rags got hold of the fact that she was a prostitute?

All relationships have a trajectory, a set of reasonable, expected steps that characterize the progression of the relationship. Stages, if you'd like. (In fact, there are five of them, as we'll learn in a moment.) While most Hollywood movies never show what happens after the first or second phase, those of us in the real world who've had one or more long-term romantic relationships have experienced the later stages. What we might not see, though, is that what we go through in relationships are specific phases that parallel our own development; how we bond with and then partially separate from the family system is remarkably similar to how we conduct our adult romantic relationships.

If you understand the unconscious forces that enable you to become attracted to someone, pursue a relationship, and eventually choose romantic commitment, then the steps of that relationship are understandable and predictable. The life cycle of the relationship looks something like this: you feel an intense attraction to someone and begin to spend time with him. Slowly, you start to suffer degrees of disappointment when you find out that he isn't everything you thought he was. You start negotiating the relationship with an eye toward feeling more satisfaction than disappointment. If you've made it this far, you'll eventually reach a point where you must decide whether the relationship is gratifying enough to push ahead into a more formally committed state, such as marriage, or whether it's time to end the relationship. (This last thing is known in intellectual circles as the "fish or cut bait" moment.)

Here are the five phases of the developing romantic relationship:

1. Attraction
2. The Honeymoon
3. Reality
   - Early Reality
   - Late Reality
4. Commitment
5. Marriage

Attraction

You're walking along the street, or looking across the room at a party, and *wham!* it happens. Or you've just opened the door and see your blind date for the first time. Or maybe instead you're out with friends and one of them has brought along someone from the office, and you immediately start looking for excuses to end the conversation you're having so you can go over and say hello. In fact, it can happen in any one of a million ways: you can feel that first moment of romantic attraction for someone in just about any setting, at pretty much any time. It is as intense as it is unexpected. Call it chemistry, if you'd like. Call it love at first sight.

But don't call it physical . . . at least, not completely. For while most of us believe that any immediate attraction we feel for someone else must be based on looks, body shape, the way that person is dressed (or a hundred other surface reasons), the truth lies a little deeper. So deep as to be on an unconscious level, actually.

Each of us carries around a set of invisible antennae that are always working, always in the process of sensing who and what the people around us really are. Obviously, there's no way of consciously "knowing" much about someone we've just met, or are about to be introduced to. We can't guess at their personality traits based on the fact that they are somehow pleasing to our eye. But we don't have to guess . . . because on an unconscious level, we sense a great deal about them; that is, we unconsciously recognize some level of compatibility between our personalities. When Tom Cruise says to Renée Zellweger, at the end of *Jerry Maguire,* "You complete me," he's making my point: attraction is the sense of having one's unconscious needs met by another person. Why else would a female friend say excitedly, "I think I met the *right* guy"? We become attracted to people, romantically, when we think they meet our needs—when they're "right" for us. That's why the experience of attraction carries with it such strong emotional feelings.

These feelings are all good, at the start. An attraction to someone else makes us feel warm, loving, excited, and aroused. We want to know the other person more fully; we want to see them and be with them. This initial stage of a relationship becomes a bonding of sorts, a bonding that's very much like the one that took place in the earliest days of life. Once again, we're experiencing the mutual good feelings that come with a caring, nurturing relationship. The difference is that since we're now adults, and already have a history of internalized relationships, there are specific things in the other person's unconscious to which our unconscious reacts.

Here's what I mean: as an adult, when you experience someone else as desirable and attractive, there is an immediate connection between that person's personality—that person's internalized experiences—and your own. If you want to know why you're drawn to someone, you have to look at what unconscious needs you have that would be filled by the relationship. Which is how you can tell a potentially positive, warm relationship from a self-destructive, cold one.

When your own personality is intact—when you're in pretty good shape emotionally—your new love object probably has certain characteristics that will add to, complement, and enhance your sense of self. And vice versa: they sense things in you that will help them, as well. Most attraction, in fact, is based on the unconscious desire to compensate for missing character traits. Next time you meet a couple about whom you remark, "Boy, they really seem to complement each other," this is what you're talking about. Maybe she brings him out of his shell; maybe he helps her to see things more positively. These are traits that they unconsciously sought out, and recognized instantly upon meeting each other.

> Most attraction, in fact, is based on the unconscious desire to compensate for missing character traits.

It works the same for the couple you just met who seem locked in an eternal battle, the couple about whom you say, "Does neither of them know the number of a good divorce attorney?" The other, decidedly negative, basis for the chemistry of personal attraction is the need to produce or perform a kind of defensive operation in order to maintain one's personal sense of well-being. In other words, if a person needs to constantly project a piece of his personality into another in order to protect himself from anxiety, he might seek out a partner who unconsciously carries some trace of that same piece. Then he can use the process of projective identification to make the other person experience and manifest that negative trait, so that he can constantly convince himself that it's his partner who's defective, and not himself.

The reasons for personal attraction, whether positive or negative, are as diverse and complicated as the personalities involved, but the nature of the attraction is always the same: the people involved see within each other personality elements that will help them in some way.

Romantic attraction can begin virtually immediately—across a crowded room—or it can happen on a delayed basis. There are times when long-standing friendships turn into romantic relationships. (*When Harry Met Sally,* anyone?) What's interesting to note about these latter relationships, the ones that evolve over time, is . . . well, I'll tell you about it by way of a little classroom demonstration that Bernie conducts each semester. First, Bernie finds students who have had a friendship turn into a love relationship. This isn't hard, because even at a relatively early age, most of us have experienced a friend becoming something more. Then Bernie asks a basic question: "Aside from the addition of the physical stuff, what changes in the relationship?" Each semester, he hears some version of the same two replies: "When we're friends, I trust her completely" and "When we're lovers, there are times when he makes me feel insecure and jealous." His students go on to explain that what they lose when a friendship becomes a romance is the feeling that they can communicate almost anything to each other, without any need to keep secrets or tell lies.

Oddly enough, Bernie's students tell him, when a relationship becomes more intimate in nature, the emotional change seems largely negative: there is a decrease in trust, a growing unwillingness (or inability) to communicate honestly, and a new capacity for jealousy, insecurity, and rejection. They also invariably report that trust decreases when a friendship becomes a romance, while emotional intensity grows . . . which can be a good thing and a bad thing. Okay, mostly a bad thing: the major difference between friendship and love, Bernie's students tell him, is that the intense emotions they experience most commonly are anger, jealousy, and anxiety.

> The major difference between friendship and love, Bernie's students tell him, is that the intense emotions they experience most commonly are anger, jealousy, and anxiety.

How can that be, they want to know, when love is supposed to be a much deeper, more satisfying bond than friendship? Well, it is a deeper bond, Bernie tells them . . . but the "more satisfying" part can be tricky.

That's because the chemistry part of romantic attraction isn't just some random thing; it isn't some physiological or genetically based instinct. Instead, it has to do with a "playing out" of unconscious forces that began forming during our earliest internalized relationships. The feeling of being attracted to someone, romantically, has specific causes for each of us—which is why we don't become attracted to everyone we meet—and those causes are directly related to our own unique personalities. Think of it this way: *attraction,* the first phase in the life cycle of the love relationship, mirrors *symbiosis,* the first phase of the relationship an infant has with a parent. In symbiosis, the infant looks upon the parent as someone with very special and significant powers: the parent seems infallible, omnipotent, and the possessor of all that is good. It is only later on, as childhood progresses into adolescence, that a child sees a parent as a person with imperfections and weaknesses.

In the attraction phase, what we're really doing is reliving the emotions and perceptions of that perfect parent we knew in our earliest days. Reality is still two phases away.

The Honeymoon

And so it begins . . . welcome to *idealized positive transference,* the second stage of the relationship. (I cheated a little when I chose "the honeymoon" for the name of this phase. I'm sorry, but it's just much sexier than "idealized positive transference.") Now that we've found someone to whom we're attracted, it's time to idealize her or him a little. To do that, we'll first turn inward, and consult that standard of perfection— that picture of the ideal mate—we've been carrying around in our unconscious. We can "see" those perfect people in our head, and we can "feel" them, too: whether we seek a man or a woman, romantically, we may have strong ideas of what our perfect mate will look like, how they'll treat us, how we'll feel about them, what traits they'll have, and so on. This inner notion of perfection is something that we've been working on since our infancy, when we first bonded with a parent.

Again, we first experience our parents as perfect; they are the source of all gratification. This is because we meet them long before we develop any intellectual, objective capacity to assess or judge them in a realistic way. And so it is in this second phase of our romantic relationship: we see the person we're getting involved with as perfect, omnipotent, and the source of immense gratification. Now, we should know better by this point in our lives, seeing as how we're adults and as such have developed the ability to think rationally. Well, forget rationality: as Woody Allen so famously said, "The heart wants what it wants." When it comes to choosing a romantic object, our fantasies and unconscious pictures of "the perfect person" ultimately have the most say. Early on in a relationship, our lack of any real knowledge of our new partner couples with our desire to please, and further interferes with any realistic assessment of his or her strengths and weaknesses.

The term *idealized positive transference,* then, is relatively simple to understand. The "idealized" part we've just looked at: it's that image we hold in our unconscious of what we'd imagine the perfect person to be. This is our idealized romantic partner. The "positive" part refers to the fact that—at first—everything we experience of the new person in our life can be ascribed to all those perfect, positive attributes we're sure they've got. Like love, attention, affection, and whatever else it is that makes us feel good. Finally, we come to a process: transference. In psychological terms, transference is the unconscious act of taking your feelings about one person and projecting them onto another. (Shrinks most commonly use transference to describe what happens when a patient starts feeling about the shrink the way she feels about her parents.) Idealized positive transference, then, is the process through which you take that unconscious, wholly optimistic idea of "the perfect mate" and project it onto someone for whom you feel the chemistry of romantic attraction. In other words, it's the act of seeing someone not for who they are, but for who you want them to be.

Now that you've transferred the ideal out of your unconscious and onto your new love, the feelings you have for them are overwhelmingly positive. You feel attraction, attentiveness, warmth, consideration, thoughtfulness, and the like. And how could you not? For the moment, you're in love with your ideal . . . you're in love with a fantasy, not a person. During this phase of the relationship, you really don't have much idea of what the other person is like in terms of consistent behavior patterns, psychological makeup, or their relationships with other people. You don't yet know their romantic background. Just the same, you're willing to suspend reality in order to cherish that unconscious hope that you've met your ideal. At this point, in other words, your relationship is based more on what you desire than on what the reality is.

Which is at it should be. Idealized positive transference is an absolutely critical phase in any potential long-term romantic relationship. This is the bonding phase, the time during which you build a connection that will have to be strong enough to withstand the (inevitable) disappointments that will appear in the next phase.

Remember that feedback loop we talked about in the last chapter, where a parent and child feel, amplify, and return each other's feelings? Well, we're back at it. The initial stages of a relationship work the same way; positive projective identifications are bouncing back and forth, creating good, warm, and loving feelings between you and your new partner. In effect, if there were too much "reality" in the first few stages of your relationship, your chances of creating a long-term relationship would be low at best; were critical thinking and negative projections to start at this point, your budding romance might well wither. You bond to your romantic love object with the same psychological blinders on that you wore when you bonded with your parent right after birth: you had no idea if your mom was Mother Teresa or Lizzie Borden, but you loved her completely all the same. You bond because it's what your psyche needs for you to do, first with your parent and then with your partner.

Idealized positive transference, the honeymoon phase of your relationship, can last from a few months to as long as several years, depending upon the amount of physical and emotional separation you experience. Move in together right away, and the honeymoon fades much more quickly. Conduct your love affair from distant cities, and the honeymoon may last longer than your ability to pay your long-distance phone bill. What will happen as the relationship continues is that each person starts to experience the reality of who the other person is. That reality—your discovery that he's a little too creepily attached to his mother, for instance—will begin to erode the idealized positive transference you've been conducting.

One of the fascinating things to notice about this kind of transference is how it affects what you're willing to accept and tolerate in your partner. It's a sliding scale: the stronger the idealization, the more you're able to accept . . . and the more you're able to reveal about yourself with almost virtual impunity.

For instance, very early on in a relationship, you might very well be able to tell your new boyfriend or girlfriend that you're wanted in several states, for crimes you'd rather not talk about. At this point, you might even get away with the admission; you might have your new love thank you for your honesty, and he or she could actually come away from the conversation feeling wonderful about being involved with someone who is able to be so open and honest. Try telling your partner the same thing a couple of phases farther down the relationship road, and you'd likely get a much different reaction, if you're not dropped off at the nearest police precinct.

A patient of Bernie's once told a new girlfriend that he didn't bathe. He said he felt washing and cleaning were merely the demands of society, and as an individualist and nonconformist he wouldn't be told what to do. As they'd only been dating for several weeks, she responded with delight: how great to have met a man with such strong self-esteem! "Most men," she told her new boyfriend, "are such sheep. They're only too willing to go along with the masses." As Bernie predicted at the time, though, she ultimately decided the masses weren't wrong when it came to personal cleanliness. After several months she began to complain about his smell, and gave him a choice: "Take a shower, or lose me forever."

This kind of early acceptance of just about anything is a strong part of idealized projection, and as such, is affected by proximity: again, if you live close by and see each other frequently, your ability to overlook negative traits in your partner is shorter-lived. It might last three to six months. If you don't see much of each other, because you live far away or you're simply too busy, this idealized, positive stage can last much longer, because reality doesn't get much of a chance to be introduced into your relationship.

When I asked Bernie for an example of the latter, a relationship that used distance to keep the positive transference going, he told me this story:

A couple meet in a nightclub in New York City. She lives and works in the city, but he's only in town on vacation; he actually lives and works several hours away in Buffalo. They're both in their late twenties, and both have excellent jobs and careers. Each is highly resistant to the idea of moving for the sake of a relationship. Still, they have an immediate attraction for each other and begin the idealized positive transference stage before he has to go home and back to work. They agree to continue seeing each other, building a relationship in which they'll speak often, they'll write to each other, and try to visit with some regularity.

As the relationship progresses, they settle into a routine. They talk on the phone a few times a week, and see each other every other weekend. After a few years of this, they marry. In fact, they've been married for a dozen years now, and still manage candlelit dinners every weekend. They rarely argue. They talk openly and honestly to this day.

"Come on, Bernie," I said. "You're telling me that a few years of separation early on kept the honeymoon going indefinitely, even twelve years after the separation gave way to marriage?" That's when he hit me with the punch line to this true story: "Who said they moved in together?" The couple, it turns out, still live apart, most of the time. They keep separate residences and bank accounts; basically, each lives as a single person. Bernie's point is that reality still hasn't had a chance to intrude upon their lives. Should they eventually move in together, he says . . . well, then all bets are off.

For most of us, this phase of a relationship has a far shorter life span. During its early days, we experience an on-going and continuing set of good feelings about the person we're with, and a strong desire for them. As the relationship progresses and reality is introduced, though, we start to feel some degree of disappointment with our partner. He or she may have behaviors, habits, attitudes, values, and friends that bother us in some way. No need to panic, though: if reality is introduced gradually but still within the idealized transference phase, chances are good we can come up with some tolerance for our partner's disappointing features. With the idealization still going on, our disappointments seem minimal in relation to our strong, positive feelings.

Here's the important thing to keep in mind about the idealized positive transference phase of a romantic relationship: it's a lousy time to make any serious decisions. As much as entering into a long-term commitment such as marriage may seem like a terrific idea among all these good feelings, it isn't. The problem with making such a leap too early in the relationship is that it's a decision based on a projection, and not on a realistic reflection of who the other person is. Impulsively marrying during this phase can end in disaster, because it introduces reality into the relationship in an abrupt, almost overwhelmingly powerful way . . . so the idealizations aren't slowly eroded, but rather shattered all at once. Too much negativity, too soon, is a terrible way to start married life.

Starting to understand why a little idealization is a good thing? Idealized positive transference is best understood as a framework for a relationship, within which it's possible to slowly accept and tolerate the disappointments that are inevitable: in plain English, this phase gives us a chance to get to know a potential life partner, free (so far) of the stresses of reality. With a solid bond, created by a sufficiently lengthy period of idealization, the shifts of emotion that occur when reality starts to intrude don't feel like "falling *out* of love," but rather as the natural consequence of being with someone for an extended period of time.

Reality

There's a very simple way of knowing when you're out of the idealized transference phase and into the reality phase of your relationship: it's the moment when you first realize that your new partner isn't perfect. It's the moment when you finally discover something about your lover that you just don't like. Once you've hit that sad (but necessary) moment, you're entering into the reality phase, which is really two phases— early reality and late reality.

Early Reality

If you'll check your rearview mirror, you'll notice that the Garden of Eden is now behind you, and getting smaller. That's because you've just found something about the person you're attracted to that isn't very attractive, and you've started to lose your ability to excuse or rationalize pretty much anything that person is or does. While you were still in the idealization phase, you'd encounter something negative in your partner and immediately diminish its importance. You'd repress it, deny it, or rationalize it. ("Okay, so he's *always* late . . . but he's completely adorable when he apologizes!") In fact, you were so good at this that the bad stuff you encountered would be forgotten within a day or two. Now, though . . . now it's not so easy. You've started to wake up and smell the defects. In the early part of the reality phase, the behavior patterns in your partner that you feel negatively toward can no longer be swept under the rug. Now they're full-fledged concerns, and as they're mounting, your tolerance for them seems to be waning.

Now's the time for communication, because it's very important to tell your partner about the things that are distressing you. And here's the good news: there are enough good feelings stored up from the previous phase of your relationship—the positive transference phase—that you'll probably find a willingness in your partner to deal with and work on those things. This is the time when compromise and change are the most possible. During this overlap between idealization and reality, each of us is more willing to hear what the other is saying in terms of where the difficulties in your relationship lie. (Now's the time when you're both most likely to communicate without seeming overly critical or attacking, which certainly helps.)

The early-reality phase of a relationship is the time when your negative feelings toward your partner exist, but seem far outweighed by your positive feelings; it's when the good stuff is felt more frequently and more intensely than the bad stuff. As long as this equation continues—the good trumps the bad—the relationship has a good chance of continuing.

If there are two words that best sum up the early-reality phase, they are *acceptance* and *risk*. Once you're out of the garden of idealization and into the forest of reality, you start to accept that nothing (and no one, not even your lover) is perfect. You take responsibility for the belief that your relationship is going to work or fail depending on the strengths and weaknesses each of you possess, and you no longer automatically assume that things will go as well as they once did. The risk comes when you actually have to act on this new reality, and make your first attempts at communicating things to your partner that may be unpleasant to hear. For the first time, you're risking a potentially negative response, and quite possibly rejection. You're finding out how the two of you will deal with conflict resolution, which is absolutely critical to the progression of your relationship: if you can't work stuff out in the present, there's no point in planning for the future.

> Once you're out of the garden of idealization and into the forest of reality, you start to accept that nothing (and no one, not even your lover) is perfect.

In the early-reality phase of your relationship, you'll most likely find that you can handle those first bouts of negativity . . .

Late Reality

. . . but that doesn't mean you should get too comfortable just yet.

Eventually (and inevitably) you'll hit that moment when you wonder for the very first time if your relationship is the right one for you, or if it's best that you moved on. Such a moment comes when the negatives have piled up a bit—when you see them as being almost equal to or even greater than the positive aspects of your bond with your lover. This first moment of doubt doesn't mean that the relationship isn't going well, and it certainly doesn't mean that it has to end, but it does mean you've graduated from the early phase of reality and entered the late phase. It means that reality has finally and fully caught up with idealization.

In the late-reality phase, your eyes are completely open. You can see the faults your partner has, just as they can see yours. Still, there are enough remnants of all those idealized feelings you shared in the earlier phases of your relationship to prompt one or both of you to express a desire to work out the problems, to compromise, and to continue to stay together. In this phase, even though there's enough conflict to cause you to wonder whether or not the relationship will last, you discover your capacity for making up, for feeling good about your partner despite your newfound fears. When you do manage to get through your first fight, or that first bout of jitters, what you'll find is that the loving, sexual feelings the relationship started with will most likely reassert themselves.

Which, when you think about it, is a pretty good motivation for continuing on in a romantic relationship. The potential rearousal of the strongly positive feelings and desires you experienced early on with someone is a strong incentive for resolving these new conflicts.

And you'll need the incentive, because the onset of the late-reality phase brings with it the first appearance of defensive and possibly chronically conflicted behavior . . . and a weakening ability to put up with that behavior. In the early-reality phase, you're far more likely (and willing) to listen to your partner's complaints calmly and to attempt to change some habit or aspect of your personality for the sake of the relationship. This isn't the case once early reality has passed you by: now you may find yourself constantly criticized—or constantly critical—and far less willing to modify your behavior.

During the late-reality phase, there is a crisis in the relationship in this sense: one or both of you may doubt the ability of the relationship to continue. But at the same time, you feel a great deal of reluctance to part. You can thank the bonding you experienced in the idealized positive transference phase for that. It's through that bonding that you've created a built-in defense for the relationship: namely, the fear that the relationship's *end* will bring with it extremely painful feelings of failure, rejection, abandonment . . . or some horrible mixture of all three. That it will cause depression and anxiety. On a deeper level, you fear that since the initial attraction and subsequent relationship were both based on the wish to fulfill unconscious needs, if you split up you'll find yourself with an unconscious void. (Ever notice how people who've just broken up describe themselves as feeling "empty" inside?)

The desire to keep a relationship going isn't just to stave off depression, of course. It also comes about because you remember what those early, positive feeling states were like and you want to get them back. So you start evaluating where you are and where you've been. Is there too much anger, anxiety, and accusation in your relationship for it to have a chance of surviving? If so, then maybe the stuff that attracted you to this person in the first place was negative . . . maybe the attraction was based on a more defensive need in you. Maybe it's time to move on.

If you find that the anxieties you're feeling in regard to your relationship don't overwhelm its positive aspects, you'll ultimately choose one of three courses: you'll repress the problems and hope they'll self-correct, or you'll attempt to deal with them through minor (or even major) compromise, or you'll look for some form of professional intervention, such as couples therapy. Whichever you choose, the simple fact that you haven't chucked the relationship out the window altogether means you've successfully moved on to your relationship's next phase: you've made a romantic commitment.

Commitment

Here's the first phase that's characterized not so much by what you're getting, but rather by what you're giving up. Namely, other people. Commitment starts when you and your partner acknowledge a wish to see each other exclusively and are ready to give up the pursuit of other romantic attractions or involvements. This is a very good sign for your relationship: after weighing the pros of the first two phases with the cons of the third, you decide to forego other romantic entanglements for the sake of determining if this one is "it."

This is the time where you begin to consciously negotiate boundaries for your relationship. You start to discuss what each of you expects from the other in terms of togetherness . . . and autonomy. It's right about now that you're most likely to hear (or say) "I need more space" or "I need more time to be with my friends." But this isn't cause for panic, really; it's a replay of the movement away from symbiosis with your parent, it's a way of saying "I know you're there, and I'm bonded to you, but I need to have a little independence." Looked at this way, the give-me-my-space phenomenon is actually pretty healthy for the relationship. If you can handle the reemergence of autonomy within your relationship, then that relationship enters a phase in which its durability complements the individual growth of each person in it, and vice versa. In other words, strong, healthy individuals make for a strong relationship, and a strong relationship makes for strong, healthy individuals.

The perfect relationship, to the degree such a thing can exist, is the one where there's just the right amount of togetherness and just the right amount of separation. It's a tricky balance, and it's not easy to achieve. Early on in a committed relationship, it's very common for a couple to fight over each partner's willingness (or lack thereof) to accept the "space" needs of the other.

> Now that the blinders are off—wiped away by the late-reality phase you just survived—you now find yourself with a new task: accepting your partner for who they are, and not for who you'd idealized them to be.

Actually, it's very common for a couple in the commitment phase to fight, period. Now that the blinders are off—wiped away by the late-reality phase you just survived—you now find yourself with a new task: accepting your partner for who they are, and not for who you'd idealized them to be.

Now's the time when it first occurs to you that the person you're with is not who you thought he or she was. Now's the time when it first occurs to you that *change* might have some role in your relationship. In other words, you've begun shifting your image of your partner away from who you imagined they were and toward who you're hoping they'll be. Estelle Getty, an actress best known for her work on *The Golden Girls,* once made a great observation about the role of change in a relationship: women marry men thinking that they're going to change them, but they never do. Men, she continued, marry women hoping that they'll never change . . . but they invariably do.

Here's a little tip from Bernie, who's counseled enough couples to know: if you enter a committed relationship with—or eventually marry—someone who will only be able to satisfy your needs after they make significant changes to their personality, you're begging for trouble.

In order to save yourself from major conflict later on— we're talking emotional nuclear warfare—now's the time that it's absolutely essential to step back and ask yourself four basic, related questions:

Who is this person I'm with?
Does he have what it takes to fulfill me emotionally?
Do our personalities mesh . . . or conflict?
Is there something I've been doing without for the sake
    of getting this far in the relationship?

The commitment phase is your last chance to make sure you're basically compatible, so it's best to be very, very honest with yourself about what you need, what you want, and what you're willing to settle for. The tricky part is that the commitment phase is also the first full phase of the relationship where you're getting a clear view of . . . what you're getting. You've taken your blinders off, and chances are good your partner is also making a little less of an effort to be who they figure you want them to be. ("You used to be *so* romantic" is a phrase that may rear its ugly head, long about now, as is "But this never used to bother you before.") In fact, there might be something very specific that you need from your partner—and used to get—but now seem to have to beg for.

Like Terry, my friend the affection junkie. When she first started dating her husband, he couldn't keep his hands off of her, which is exactly what she craved. She needed to be held, and he held her. She loved holding hands, and you'd have thought their interlocked fingers had been welded together. All through the idealization phase, into early reality, and part of the way through the late-reality stage, Stan was the huggy, touchy, affectionate man of her dreams. And then, just as she thought she'd gotten a full and accurate picture of the conflicts in their relationship, Stan stopped touching her.

Not completely, of course, but enough that she began to miss what had been a big part of their earlier relationship. Enough that she began to realize just how much she needed physical affection. In talking to Stan about it—gingerly, so as not to seem too critical—she learned that he'd been making an extra effort to give her what she wanted, but wasn't actually an affectionate guy at all, physically speaking. Because of his childhood and past romantic history, it just wasn't part of his behavioral repertoire. It felt foreign to him.

Which left Terry with two possible reactions:

1. "Okay. Stan is clearly unable to meet my needs for affection. That's part of his psychological makeup, and I can't really expect him to be someone that he isn't. I'll have to decide if I can be happy despite not getting what I need in this case."

Or

2. "That misleading *jerk*. He led me on and made me believe that he was this affectionate guy, but he isn't. Unless, of course, I can be sufficiently persuasive, critical, or just plain manipulative. Yeah, that's the ticket: I'll get what I need one way or another."

I'd write down a third possible reaction—"Oh, well, I guess he's not the guy for me"—but it would seem redundant, considering it would have meant essentially the same outcome as the second possible reaction above: the effective end of Terry and Stan as a couple. (Actually, the reaction in which Terry would manipulate, cajole, and wheedle what she wanted out of Stan wouldn't have to mean the end of the relationship. It would just mean the end to any possibility of a good, healthy relationship.) Since you're an eagle-eyed reader, you undoubtedly noticed that I started this story with, "When she first started dating her husband . . ." and you've guessed that Terry chose the first option: she came to the realization that he was so good for her in most ways that she can live with less physical affection than she had hoped for. And so far, she has.

This must all seem pessimistic, this progression of stages from the bliss of attraction to the acceptance of disappointment needed for commitment. Right about now, you're wondering if the best part of any relationship is the earliest stuff, the part that occurs between you and your partner when the blinders are on and the idealized projections are floating in the air between you like an endless stream of confetti. You're wondering if "not really knowing each other" is the best phase for a couple to be in. Well, wonder no more: the answer is yes, unfortunately. It's absolutely true that the progression of a relationship means disappointment and compromise, no matter what that one, insanely chipper couple you know (and we all know one just like them) tells you. The reality is that reality bites: the wonderful, positive feelings that characterize the start of a romantic relationship inevitably erode. If you're lucky, though, and realistic, there are other gratifications to be had in your committed relationship. Gratifications that you can rely upon, and that last a heck of a lot longer than your average idealized positive transference phase. Like the understanding that comes with a long-term, shared history. The frequent reactivation of the loving feelings developed in the earlier stages of the relationship. And the security of companionship with someone whose faults you know, but accept . . . and who knows and accepts *your* faults.

One of the most profound developments in a romantic relation-ship comes during the commitment phase and involves a differ-ent type of reactivation: those internalizations you developed in your earliest years now pop out and say hello to your new love. Remember the unconscious needs that attracted you to your partner in the first place? Well, now's the time they start to play a day-to-day role in your relationship. You may find that your behavior toward your partner becomes even more intimate, communicative, and loving. Then again, you might find your-self feeling more defensive, hurtful, critical, anxious, and angry. Most likely, though, you'll find a mix of positive and negative aspects appearing in both your behavior and your partner's.

Here's what's happening: you're both unconsciously in-dulging in a little projective identification. As we discussed in the previous chapter, projective identification is the process by which you take some part of yourself and put it *into* some-one else; that is, you make them feel a certain way, and then you react to that feeling. When the process is positive, it's like trading and amplifying those good feelings that you shared with your parent as a newborn. Back then, the process went something like this: when you felt contented—because you were just changed, or fed, or just generally comfy—you smiled and cooed at your mother; your smiling and cooing created good feelings in your mom, and she returned those feelings to you through soft words or her touch.

When the process is negative, of course, it's a way to get a kind of psychic relief at the expense of your partner: you make them feel something that you'd rather not feel, and then you reject them for feeling it. (For example, "Geez, you're always so angry all the time. What's wrong with you?")

Let's make this phenomenon even simpler: in the commitment phase, the *real* you comes out. That includes all of the stuff you've acquired through the internalization of experience, and all of your personality traits. If you've learned to be less than trusting in relationships, this is the phase where you'll start to distrust your partner. If the security of commitment prompts your unconscious to let loose a torrent of physical affection that had, up to this point, been held back by *in*security, then you'll start touching and hugging in a way that you hadn't before. Your anxieties and good feelings all are made manifest in the commitment phase.

Which is why it's so important to stay in the commitment phase until you're absolutely ready for the fifth and final phase, marriage. This is your last chance to pay special attention to the dimensions of your relationship that might cause chronic problems later on. This is the time to reject the classic (and classically wrongheaded) notion that "This will all get better after we're married." No, it won't. If the troubling aspects of your relationship aren't dealt with now, they'll get worse. Here's why: in the commitment phase of your relationship, you still have just enough fear of rejection and just enough residue of positive transference to keep some of your old family conflicts sufficiently repressed or minimized. Oh, they're obvious, at this point; you've stopped being able to hide your issues completely, but they still probably seem to be at manageable levels, which is why you feel they'll go away once you're married. Truth is, old internalized conflicts have a much greater tendency to damage your relationship after you've said "I do."

It may be tempting, at this point, to use the practice of "living together" to try to deal with the conflicts that have made themselves known in this phase. But as Bernie has found in his years of dealing with couples, it doesn't work: those couples he's counseled who moved in together before marrying have just as high a divorce rate (if not a little higher) than those who didn't. Can you see why? It's pretty simple: couples who don't live together *expect* a little tension after the wedding day; they see the stresses that arise when that fear of rejection evaporates and that last little bit of positive transference evaporates as the natural result of the change from living separately to living together. Couples who do live together before marriage don't expect the exchanging of vows to bring any real changes to the relationship . . . so they're blindsided when those changes inevitably come.

If you're in a committed relationship, you experience some level of conflict. That doesn't mean the relationship is bad or should end, and it doesn't portend a lousy marriage. What it means is that every single human being is raised by imperfect parents in an imperfect world, and because of this has a psychological "flashpoint" or two that can produce severe emotional reactions. (Hence the popular phrase, "*Man,* does my spouse know how to push my buttons!") Successful committed relationships are possible when those flashpoints—which we'll look at in depth in chapter 8—are generally avoided, and when the positive, affectionate ties between two people outweigh the negative ties. It's all about the ratio of satisfactions to disappointments and good feelings to hurtful feelings, really. When that ratio remains high well into the commitment phase, it may very well be time to make the ultimate commitment.

Marriage

I now pronounce you . . . to be in the final phase in the life cycle of the relationship. Marriage is the culmination of the phases that have come before; it's when the commitment borne out of attraction, idealization, and then reality is solidified by an act that is emotionally, psychologically, legally, and spiritually binding. By marrying, you create an unconscious confusion between the past and the present, because now your idea of family shifts to your partner. By marrying, you both symbolically and literally make the final break from your family of origin.

Ah, but if only your personality could make that final break. Unfortunately, it's the nature of psychological development that your personality has been formed by internalizing the good and bad from past relationships; since that's the personality you're bringing with you into marriage, those past relationships are still hanging around. The marriage of two adults is really the joining together of two personalities, each with its own fulfilling and depriving aspects.

When these personalities, thanks to a preponderance of positive childhood experiences, are solid and mature, then spouses manage to induce good feelings in each other through projective identification. That makes for a happy marriage, where supportive, happy feelings are the norm. When people with less-than-stellar histories of relating with their families get together, though . . . well, this is what keeps therapists such as Bernie in business. When the stuff that a couple is projecting into each other is mostly negative and anxiety-producing, things are bound to go badly in the marriage.

One of the things that sets the marital phase apart from the commitment phase—aside from the legal papers, of course—is the addition of a little role-playing to the relationship. Now's the time when we consciously seek to fix the things we think are wrong with us by prompting our spouse to behave in ways that our parents didn't. (Here's where that "unconscious confusion between the past and the present" that I mentioned a few paragraphs back comes into play.)

For example, let's say you had a punitive, belittling mother. Sure, you were angry with her, but you could never allow yourself to be critical of her, for fear of emotional rejection and retaliation from the all-important, all-powerful adult. Now that you're married, though, those fears are gone, and you might react very strongly to even the slightest criticism from your spouse. It's not so much that you're trying to "get back at" your mother, but rather that you're trying to goad your spouse into being the kind, understanding mom you never had. You do that because if you can get your spouse to be kind and understanding, you won't reexperience those lousy feelings your mom brought out of you when she criticized you. See how it works? We replay our past, in the hopes of fixing the things we feel are broken.

(Note the interesting contradiction in the above: when we're married, we're compelled to try to cure our relationship woes by re-creating them.)

Quite often, those needs that were not met when we were children can be complementary in marriage: for instance, your spouse might need to be nurtured, and you might need the opportunity to be nurturing. When that's the case, you give each other what you crave and you wind up feeling good about each other. If, however, one of you needs to be nurtured and the other one resents being relied upon, chances are very good the disconnect will become the source of a chronic marital problem. The strength of a marriage comes down, in large part, to the compatibility of spouses' personality traits.

> If you really think about it, marriage is a second chance, psychologically speaking. It's a second chance to get those needs met that our parents couldn't satisfy.

If you really think about it, marriage is a second chance, psychologically speaking. It's a second chance to get those needs met that our parents couldn't satisfy. If those unsatisfied needs are great, we've experienced what shrinks call "primary maturational failure," and we eventually look to our spouse to fill them. If our spouse has trouble filling those needs, we can become extraordinarily angry and critical—that's our internalized experience rearing its ugly head—and pretty much guarantee that our spouse will stop trying to help us. This, of course, is "secondary maturational failure," and it's the cause of many a divorce. The important thing to remember is that when a person says they feel "blind-sided" by the psychological demands of a spouse and the anger that comes when those demands aren't met, they ain't just whistlin' "Dixie"—these demands and behaviors are *triggered* by the act of marriage.

If you're having a hard time believing just how differently a personality functions within a married relationship, then think about the marital arguments you've heard (or experienced) where some version of the following is said: "How come nobody else criticizes me but you?" Or maybe you've heard, "No one else seems to have a problem with my _____." (Fill in the blank with anything from "singing" to "questions" to "outfit.") It's not so uncommon that the person who is perceived as Mr. Nice Guy by just about everyone outside his home is actually abusive and tyrannical to his own wife and children. It's not so uncommon that the woman who is known for being caring and nurturing, who will go out of her way for friends and strangers alike, goes home and refuses to do the simplest thing requested by her husband. Folks like these have a little bit of a split personality going on: inside the home, they're re-creating the worst traits of their parents, and outside the home, they're showing their "adaptive face," the one they created so that they could *survive* their parents' worst traits.

When you picture the people in your life who fit the above description, the ones who seem chronically locked in some marital battle, you inevitably come to one question: "Why the heck are they still together?" The answer is simple: their situation is complex.

Each marriage has relative degrees of happiness and conflict. When the psychological needs mesh and are complementary, happiness wins out. It's when both spouses have, as part of their primary unconscious agenda, the need to change each other in order to get something from the other that they couldn't get from their own families, that the marriage is mostly conflicted. But that ongoing conflict is also a funny—funny weird, not funny ha-ha—kind of bond between them. You've heard the phrase "the ties that bind"? Well this is a bind that ties, because each person is desperate to get that thing they needed in their earliest days, and they're convinced that the only person who might, with the right coaxing, be able to give it to them is their spouse. They're convinced of this as a result of those halcyon days back in the first few phases of the relationship, when they were busy imbuing their spouse with idealized qualities and having wonderful feelings toward him or her.

So the relationship becomes its own negative feedback loop, and there are a whole lot of factors driving the (downward) spiral. There are the childhood needs that are not getting met. There is the desire to reactivate all of that good stuff from the early days of the relationship. There is the ingrained belief—created during the idealization phase—that the spouse is the only one who might be able to meet those needs *and* be the source of good feelings. There is frustration and anger when the spouse doesn't manage to do those things. There is also the reemergence of separation anxiety; that is, the fear of the depression that might be caused by a divorce. Add up the elements of a chronically conflicted marriage, and you've got yourself a great little recipe for misery.

For most of us, the experience of marriage lies somewhere on the vast plain between the bliss of ideal(ized) circumstances and the torture of unending conflict. The positive and negative aspects of marriage—the final phase in the life cycle of the relationship—are dependent upon the positive and negative aspects of the personalities involved . . . aspects that were formed in early childhood. Those aspects create feedback loops of feelings projected between spouses, feelings that can be positive or negative.

But you're not reading this book to learn about the *range* of relationship experiences: you're trying to figure out how healthy your own relationship is, and what you can do to minimize the conflict within it. So let's do that. Let's move forward with the understanding that, while we all experience some negative feedback loops in a long-term love relationship, it's really a matter of degrees. After decades of counseling couples, Bernie has learned that conflict comes in four sizes: low, moderate, high, and severe. In the next chapter, we'll see what each of those stages of marital conflict looks like, and we'll figure out what shape *your* romantic partnership is in.

Are you ready to take the Relationship Stress Test?

5.

The Relationship
Stress Test

I have a friend, Bobby, who is so insanely logical that he can figure all the angles on just about anything. From a home purchase to a legal case, the guy knows exactly which pieces of information are relevant and how to rank the probability of each potential outcome. I keep telling Bobby that he should head to Vegas, and sit at the blackjack tables for a few days. He'd own the town inside of a week. He is smart, he is rational, . . .

. . . and he is single. With a brain like Bobby's, relationships are just about impossible.

Relationships defy traditional logic, because they're not created in a vacuum, nor are they based on quantifiable, superficial characteristics. People don't end up together because they have the same hobbies, or because they meet each other's threshold for physical attractiveness. For as much as Match.com and other dating services would like to make you believe that a twenty-page questionnaire is the first step to guaranteed romantic bliss, it just isn't true: the stuff that makes a relationship possible between two people can't be ticked off a checklist . . . hell, a great deal of it can't be *identified*. Not even by the relationship's participants. Which is why relationships constantly elude Bobby. He has a hard time trusting what he can't wrap his mind around.

All romantic relationships contain the elements of our internalized past that manifest themselves in our adult personality. That includes the unconscious stuff, which is often only dredged up or activated by a developing or ongoing relationship. (In other words, while my wife really does bring out the best in me . . . every once in a while, she brings out the worst.) Because our unconscious is made up of remnants of the more distressing parts of our past, it puts negative pressure on us. It causes us to behave, and often fight, in ways that reflect our very earliest family conflicts. The distressing thing for folks like Bobby is this: even if we could manage to make our unconscious somehow conscious, even if we could understand what it is that makes us happy or sets us off, there is no way on earth of knowing what a potential partner's unconscious is like—and how it will mesh (or not) with ours—until the relationship has progressed way past casual dating.

Fortunately, the steps that make up the life cycle of the relationship usually help us weed out the partners who are completely wrong for us. Once the idealization phase has run its course, and we experience the early- and late-reality phases, we start to see the relationship clearly enough to make realistic choices: "Sure, he's great with my parents and friends, but am I going to marry someone who says he doesn't want kids?" or maybe "It's great that she's so driven in her career, but I don't see myself with someone who's so critical of *my* plans." There are far more breakups than there are relationships, because most of us are able to understand basic incompatibilities and act on them.

Commitment, then, and ultimately marriage, come only after we've successfully negotiated the earlier phases of the relationship, and are theoretically compatible enough to move forward. It's in these later phases that consistent patterns of interaction emerge: how we talk to each other, treat each other, and react to each other is something that develops over time. Our patterns of interaction always have both positive and negative elements in them—even that "perfect couple" you know fights *some*times— and the relative health of a relationship depends upon the ratio: if the interaction is mostly positive, things are good. If the interaction is mostly bad . . . well, that's why we have marriage counselors and divorce lawyers.

> Our patterns of interaction always have both positive and negative elements in them—even that "perfect couple" you know fights sometimes—and the relative health of a relationship depends upon the ratio: if the interaction is mostly positive, things are good.

If you can remember back to high-school math, you probably have some recollection of what a graph with an *x* and a *y* axis looks like, and how it works. (If you don't remember, just imagine a big *L,* where the horizontal part is as long as the vertical part. That vertical part is the *x* axis, and the horizontal part is the *y* axis. Is it coming back to you now?) Graphs help us to plot out the relationship of two variables—the *x*

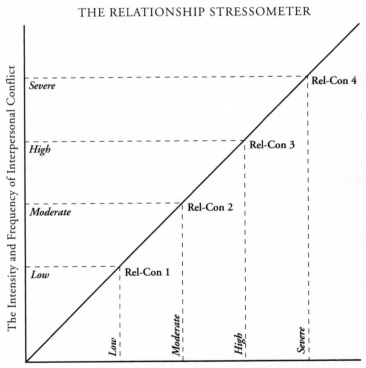

THE RELATIONSHIP STRESSOMETER

The Intensity and Frequency of Interpersonal Conflict

Severe — Rel-Con 4

High — Rel-Con 3

Moderate — Rel-Con 2

Low — Rel-Con 1

Low *Moderate* *High* *Severe*

The Degree to Which One Partner's Needs Cause Emotional Stress in the Other Partner and the *y*—and in our case, can make a nice little visual point about the state of a romantic relationship. In fact, here's our graph now: the Relationship Stressometer.

As you can see, the *x* axis—the vertical line—represents the intensity and frequency of interpersonal conflict . . . or, how often and how badly we fight with our romantic partner. The *y* axis—the horizontal line—stands for the degree to which one partner's needs cause emotional distress in the other partner, which doesn't need any explanation. The spot at which the two axes meet represents the starting point for both lines . . . that is, zero fighting and zero stress. (In other words, Fantasyland.) At intervals up or along each axis, we have four distinct points: low, moderate, high, and severe. On the *x* axis, those points stand for different levels of conflict, from low to severe, and on the *y* axis, those points stand for the amount of emotional distress each partner in a relationship feels, based on the needs of the other . . . so "low" would mean minimal distress, "moderate" would mean average distress, and so on.

Notice that line drawn at a 45-degree angle? That's where the points on each axis meet. It's a line we call the relationship gradient, and it's the line on which we'll find *your* relationship. By matching the corresponding points on each axis—a low level of fighting with a low level of distress, and so forth—we come up with four points along the relationship gradient. Those four points are the four basic conditions of a romantic relationship, in terms of conflict. You know how the military uses def-con, short for "defensive condition," to describe the level of alert our armed forces are on at any given time? Well, we'll swipe that idea, and refer to each point on our gradient as a Rel-Con, for "relationship condition." (Military purists will note that I've reversed the numbering: Rel-Con Four is the equivalent of—and just about as dangerous as—def-con one.)

We're going to take a look at each of the four basic levels of conflict before going on, in the next chapter, to look at what you can do to improve the condition of *your* relationship, no matter what its level of conflict.

Rel-Con One: What You Need You Get . . . What They Need, You Give

In a level one relationship condition, things—romantically speaking—are about as good as they come. Each partner causes minimal stress in the other, and consequently there is a minimal amount of fighting going on. Relationships like this are the result of tremendously good partner selection on both sides of the equation: each person has chosen, in the other, someone who meets both their conscious and unconscious needs, and gets good feelings by doing so. Here's an example of a couple experiencing Rel-Con One, from Bernie's practice:

The Petersons have been married for fifteen years, and are both in their forties. Grace Peterson came from a background in which she was the primary caretaker for her very depressed mother. Why was her mother depressed? (I'm glad you ask, because it has a great deal to do with Grace's unconscious.) Grace's mother was raised in a home where almost all of the emotional and physical care was given to her brothers, and almost none to her and her sister. So Grace's mother grew up bitter about her own lack of personal success, and generally felt unfulfilled. Grace, in a way, took over the role of the parent in her relationship with her mother. She internalized the role of the nurturer; it made her happy to be able to care for her mom . . . and eventually her romantic partners.

Roger Peterson, on the other hand, wasn't the recipient of the kind of gender favoritism that was withheld from his mother-in-law. No, Roger's house was ruled by self-absorbed, narcissistic parents who didn't give much support to any of their kids. So Roger's maturational needs went unmet, and he grew up to be so dependent as to be semihelpless. Enter Grace, who grew up to be so dependable as to be almost chronically nurturing. Can you see why their relationship works so well? Roger needs to be taken care of, and receiving care gives him a satisfaction denied him in his childhood. Grace needs to be the caregiver, and meeting Roger's needs reactivates the satisfaction she felt in taking care of her mother.

Let's stick with the Petersons for just a moment longer, because there's another point to be made about the psychological preconditions that foster level one relationships. That point is pretty simple: the more unconscious resentment we carry from our childhood, the less likely we are to achieve romantic bliss. Notice how I didn't tell you that Grace *resented* the fact she had to take care of her unhappy mom? That doesn't mean that she didn't feel angry about it—she missed out on a great deal of what you and I would consider routine childhood pursuits—but rather that there was sufficient reward for her efforts at the time so that she never grew resentful. The payoff for Grace was that she was successful; her nurturing produced a good result in her mother (it made her less depressed), and her mother was able in her happier moments to nurture Grace right back. Grace's anger at missing out on things was easily outweighed by the emotional gratification she got from her relationship with her mother. For Grace, good feelings came as the result of nurturing, so she internalized the role . . . and went on to perform it for Roger, who also rewards her efforts with good feelings.

Now let's imagine, instead, what would have happened if Grace's early efforts at nurturing her depressed mom had been met differently. Let's say that rather than receiving nurturing in return, Grace's caregiving had been met with criticism or personal attack. Let's say she had been a complete failure at improving her mom's unhappy state. Were these things the case, chances are good she and Roger wouldn't be doing so well today.

Here's why: if you change the ratio between anger and satisfaction in Grace's story so that she felt far *more* anger and far *less* satisfaction as a child, you create the preconditions for lingering, unconscious resentment. Had her efforts on her mom's behalf been rebuffed or criticized, she would have had intense feelings of frustration, disappointment, and deprivation, and—here's the important thing—had no outlet for them. How could she risk expressing these things to an already depressed *and* critical mother? That would *guarantee* the elimination of any possibility of getting her needs met, and a child won't risk that. In our hypothetical, what Grace would internalize would be the *frustrating, withholding mother* and the *frustrated, angry child.*

Which would mean she'd have a far different reaction to Roger, later on. Not only would she *not* feel good about nurturing Roger—remember, nurturing brings her no satisfaction—but she'd actually be angry at and critical of Roger for needing to be nurtured in the first place. She would also be angry with him for not being able to nurture, for which she'd have an unconscious need. In the marriage, Grace would in effect *become* the *frustrating, withholding mother,* and Roger would become the *frustrated, angry child.* In other words, our hypothetical Mr. and Mrs. Peterson would find their relationship much farther out on the Relationship Stressometer.

There are an unlimited amount of personality combinations that can result in Rel-Con One. The important thing that characterizes all of them is that they be complementary: what you need, you get, and what they need, you give. Happily. Let's look at two more examples from Bernie's case files and then move on.

• Bill was the "perfect child." He was hardworking, focused, and obedient. He did well in school, never stayed out past his curfew, and was obedient. Wait—have I mentioned "obedient," yet? Actually, Bill was *so* willing to take direction from his teachers, coaches, and friends that they all must secretly have thought he didn't have a mind of his own. And thanks to parents who were both loving *and* insistent upon total control over Bill, the description was accurate: he wasn't much able to think for himself or make decisions. Enter Alice, who grew up hardworking, motivated, orderly, structured . . . and controlling.

As their relationship grew from commitment into marriage, Bill increasingly looked to Alice for guidance, which it pleased her to give. Now, when it comes to questions about money, social matters, the possibility of having children, and just about everything else, Bill defers to Alice because he doesn't know how to approach difficult decisions himself. But rather than feel controlled and helpless, Bill feels loved and nurtured by Alice's take-charge approach to their relationship, because he's reexperiencing his relationship with his nurturing-but-controlling parents. Alice doesn't think less of Bill for needing the guidance, either, she's grateful that he fulfills her need to be in control.

• Charlie suffers from chronic depression. With some regularity, he feels sad, hopeless, pessimistic, and even despairing. When he feels these things, he sits alone in a darkened room for hours at a time. His wife, Donna, is a nervous, insecure woman who lost both parents early in her life, and grew up in a succession of foster homes. Cleaning house became a coping mechanism of sorts for Donna: whenever she felt alone or rejected, she would try to gain some emotional closeness by helping some member of her foster family with the household chores.

Doesn't sound like the recipe for a low-stress marriage, but surprisingly, it is. Here's what happens between Charlie and Donna: when Charlie suffers a bout of depression and closes himself up in a dark room, Donna starts to feel anxiety. She deals with that anxiety in the way she always has: by performing some act of cleaning in proximity to the person she wants to feel close to . . . which means she goes into Charlie's dark room and starts tidying up. Her physical closeness—and lowered anxiety—makes Charlie a bit less depressed, and in his grati-tude, he starts a conversation with Donna, which further de-creases her anxiety. Now she smiles and feels calm, and behaves in a loving, supportive way, which makes Charlie feel even bet-ter. It's a positive feedback loop, and it makes for a solid bond between two people who have higher degrees of emotional neediness than most of us.

Rel-Con Two: More Positive Than Negative

As my favorite television chef says, it's time to kick it up a notch. Level two is slightly elevated from the first relationship condition in terms of conflict. At this level, each spouse has to make a bit more of an effort to compromise in order to maintain marital harmony. This means that there are times of mild discomfort, where each partner experiences the other as somewhat more disappointing and frustrating than they'd bargained for.

The key phrase here is "a little." In Rel-Con Two, the pos-itive feelings still outweigh the negative feelings. If you asked someone on this level to characterize their marriage, they'd say something like "You know, we have our moments . . . but by and large we're pretty happy." What they mean is that, while there's some amount of disagreement and probably even some chronic (that is, steady) area of conflict, the part-ners still get along, want to maintain a good relationship, and are able to show affection to each other. They see their bond as strong and positive. They just wish they didn't have to compromise quite so much. Again, this is the calling card of the level two relationship: the need to make compromises and adjustments.

Here are four examples of level two relationships, meant to illustrate the mild—but very real—level of stress they hold in store:

• Edward—like my friend Bobby—is Mr. Rational. He's great at problem-solving and uses logic and intellect with ease. Emotions, though, he hasn't a clue about. Take him to a movie, and he can hold forth at great length, afterward, about the film's plot mechanics, direction, and what debt it may or may not owe to similar movies that have come before. Just don't ask him how he "feels" about the movie, because he'll have no idea how to answer you. His wife, Francesca, on the other hand, won't care a whit for the technical aspects of the movie but will be able to tell you exactly where she laughed or cried, and will probably do so in a loud, expressive voice.

Which will prompt Edward to tell her to "calm down." And Francesca will; this is a request she's used to. In fact, this is their one chronic problem area. Edward says that when his wife is emotionally expressive—when she laughs loudly, becomes noticeably angry or nervous, or cries—he feels "assaulted" by her "intensity" and he "cannot listen." So he shushes her, and she controls herself . . . and resents her husband. But because the instances where Francesca shows a heightened level of emotion around Edward are rare, the couple still describe themselves as "happy."

• Sometimes, the chronic issue in a relationship is a one-way street. Take Greg and Henry, domestic partners who have been together for a decade, as an example. Both have thriving careers in different fields, and both enjoy spending their time off by going to concerts, art galleries, and plays together. One of the reasons that Greg and Henry were initially drawn to each other is that each is an accomplished problem-solver: in fact, Greg handles public relations crises—often for misbehaved celebrities—for a living, and he's really good at it. Henry runs the human resources department for a law firm, and he must be doing it well, because every year they give him a healthy raise.

In fact, their mutual area of professional expertise makes their chronic relationship woe a little ironic. As you can imagine, each man, when the other becomes anxious or depressed about something, launches into problem-solver mode; he searches for the cause of his partner's unhappiness and attempts to fix or solve it, whatever it is. Which works really well when Greg is the one who's depressed. It *doesn't* work so well when Henry is the one experiencing anxiety, because what Henry really needs at such times is empathy and coddling . . . two things that Greg, because he was raised by withholding parents, doesn't know how to give. Even though one of the qualities that drew Henry to Greg in the first place was Greg's ability to calmly "fix" things, it's that very same ability that Henry resents when he's depressed. Which, in turn, makes Greg—the man who can fix anything—feel like a failure. Because Henry is not often depressed, and because their relationship works very well in just about every other regard, this is a low-level—though still chronic—aspect of the partners' relationship.

• Here's a common recipe for recurring relationship stress: the partygoer marries the happy-at-homer. For Vincent and Jessica, nights out at restaurants, exotic vacations, and a steady stream of social occasions were all part of the courtship, and both seemed to enjoy their packed social life. Until they married, and bought a house. Suddenly, Jessica switched on her inner Norm—you know, the guy from *This Old House*—and began filling her time with domestic projects. She fixed up bathrooms, and oversaw a kitchen remodeling. She planned the landscaping for their backyard, and spent some recent vacation time planting flowers and shrubs. At night, she is now eager to stay in their ever-improving nest. It's the source of much of her satisfaction.

All of which doesn't sit so well with Vincent, who . . . doesn't sit (still) so well. For Vincent, enjoyment comes in the form of going out, and he is beginning to feel tricked by Jessica, who he accuses of pretending to enjoy their dating life so she could get him to "settle down." (In this case, quite literally.) For her part, Jessica can't understand why Vincent can't "grow up" now that they're married: "He only wants to have a good time, so I have to handle all the responsibilities of having a home," she complains. Because Jessica does actually enjoy going out, she still agrees to do so—albeit with much less frequency—and Vincent is so grateful when she does that he makes an effort around the house. Each resents the other for what they see as deficiencies, but they're learning to give in to their partner's wants for the sake of the marriage.

• Sociability can be an issue in another way, of course, one which has absolutely nothing to do with the stay home/go out conundrum that Vincent and Jessica face. For Karen and Lee, the sociability issue is one of communication: she does, and he doesn't.

Here's how it works: Lee was always tremendously quiet, almost to the point of being noncommunicative. Now several years into his marriage, he has fallen into a pattern of evening silence. He comes home from work, has his dinner, and then sits silently in front of the television for hours. Karen is almost his polar opposite, in this regard. She's an active, talkative, highly social woman, and complains bitterly to her friends about Lee's inability to communicate. When she voices those complaints directly to Lee, he tells her that his day is stressful, and he needs to unwind. The stuff she wants to talk about, he tells her, is emotionally and intellectually unimportant to him, and the "fluff " in her conversation actually serves to annoy him, which adds to his stress.

But for all the conflict their very basic difference causes, it is also the source of some stress-*relief:* while Karen suffers from Lee's emotional and verbal withdrawal, she also unconsciously welcomes it as a respite from her upbringing in a house where she could barely get a word in edgewise. For his part, Lee feels that, though his wife's chattering bugs him, it's probably best that at least *one* person in the marriage is able to communicate.

As you'll remember, Rel-Con One—or level one—relationships are the ones in which there isn't much conflict, each partner is quick to apologize, and both can easily show affection. These are the relationships that are experienced as mutually grati-fying. Level two relationships, then, sport two major differ-ences:

1. A chronic, recurring conflict that neither person seems able to resolve. The conflict has a low inten-sity level, and appears infrequently, but nonetheless pervades the relationship.
2. A sense of disappointment and resentment at hav-ing to compromise or behave in an emotionally dis-tressing way in order to keep a partner happy and maintain harmony in the relationship.

Rel-Con Three: More Negative Than Positive

Show me a level two relationship where the partners are ignoring their issues or expecting them to go away on their own over time, and I'll show you a level three relationship in the making. Guaran-*damn*-teed, as the old lady who lived down the street used to say.

Level three relationships, properly understood, are just like the ones in level two, except for that little jump in the misery index. (The little jump is usually caused by mounting frustration when that level two situation doesn't get better.) The basic description is very similar: relationships that fall into Rel-Con Three are the ones where compromise is neces-sary, there are periods of disagreement and discomfort, and there's some sense of disappointment within the relationship. Now, though, the negative feelings have started to predominate, and as a result the conflicts increase in intensity and frequency. There are recurring, escalating arguments that always seem to revolve around the same issues. The capacity each of the partners has to cope with all the conflict gets strained to the point where the stress feels chronic. This is the relationship condition where tempers get set off easily, remarks are often misinterpreted, and the insults fly with awful regularity.

All of which plays hell with those positive feelings from earlier in the relationship.

Couples in level three relationships can still have a good time together, and can still be affectionate toward each other. In other words, sex isn't out of the question, just yet. But what's been interesting to Bernie over the years is how much of a role vacation time plays in softening some of the stresses of a level three relationship: it's as if the chance to run away from the normal stresses and strains of "real life"— like jobs and chores and responsibilities—enables people to recover many of the good feelings they felt toward their partner early on.

Think of level three, then, as the danger zone: while relationship repair is still possible, now's the time when one or both of the partners might engage in behavior that could ultimately destroy the union. Like having affairs, or dressing each other down in public. Now's the time when each partner might try to embarrass and humiliate the other in front of friends and family; in level three relationships, arguments and unpleasant discussions have a way of moving beyond the privacy of the bedroom and into places where they can be witnessed by children . . . which in turn makes the conflict a *family* issue.

It won't surprise you to know that level three is the first one we've looked at where the word *dysfunctional* can be used to describe the relationship. People experiencing this level see their relationships as unhappy and dissatisfying, and may start to say (or at least fantasize) that "I picked the wrong person for a partner. We should never have gotten married/moved in together." This is when separation and divorce become serious considerations. The overriding issue in a level three relationship is that the partners' coping mechanisms are seriously strained, and bad feelings now predominate the bond.

Some years back, I watched a couple that my wife and I had grown close to make the leap from a level two to a level three relationship. It wasn't pretty. Rick and Dana had entered into a marriage while still in a hard-partying stage of life: Rick was well into his thirties when he met his wife in the kind of bar where "closing time" coincides with the rising of the sun. Though I didn't know them when they met, both admitted to an amazing amount of volatility in their relationship from their earliest days together. Rick used to joke that the harder they fought, the better their inevitable "makeup" sex would be.

Somewhere along the line—unfortunately after the birth of their kids—they stopped making up. The upending of their marital balance (from mostly tranquil with infrequent, nasty squabbling to mostly nasty squabbling with infrequent bouts of tranquility) came partly as a result of Rick's inability to hold a steady job or put any money away for his boys' college fund. Dana started ignoring and avoiding her husband, and he in turn grew more desperate in his efforts to get her attention. He started saying provocative things about what he'd do if he were single again. His clothing choices became . . . interesting: I still remember going to meet him at a neighboring Starbucks, and being shocked to find him standing on the street corner, waiting for me in sneakers and a tiny pair of running shorts. When I said, "Uh, dude, I think they require shirts inside," he reached around and pulled out a tank top that he'd wedged in his shorts. This was a (by then) fifty-year-old guy, acting and dressing like a member of the junior high track team.

Oh, and he started to show a teenager's volatility, too, which was one area where he was matched by his wife. Loud arguments between Rick and Dana became the norm, arguments that scared their friends and children for both the sheer decibel-level of the yelling and the physical proximity of the combatants: Rick and Dana liked to scream at each other from about six inches away. Once in awhile—usually after a few glasses of wine—Dana would even reach across those six inches and slap at Rick.

The weird part, for those of us watching the deterioration of the marriage, was that no one outside their little circle of two could criticize them: say a disparaging thing about Dana to Rick, and he'd angrily defend her. Tell Dana that perhaps they should think about splitting up, and she'd launch into a full defense of her husband, making excuses for his various and glaring failures. I guess there was another weird part, as well: every so often either Rick or Dana would make a grand romantic gesture toward the other. Rick might book a spa get-away (which they could ill-afford, a fact that would invariably lead to yet another fight) or Dana might get the kids out of the house and serve a candlelit meal for two. In this way—with fighting the norm and affectionate gestures the rarity—their marriage continued on for several years.

Couples like Rick and Dana often end up on couches like Bernie's, and when I told him about them, he rattled off a number of similar stories of level three relationships. Not surprisingly, family finances often become the focal point for the disappointments and resentments that characterize Rel-Con Three:

• For Mike, a forty-five-year-old man, responsibility is a bore. He's a procrastinator and a neglectful man who wants nothing to do with mundane stuff like household chores. He'd rather go bowling with his friends, or to ball games. He talks on the phone with old high-school pals for hours, reliving the glory days. His wife Nancy, on the other hand, is a highly controlled, hardworking woman who manages every aspect of their household. To Nancy, Mike isn't a partner but a burden: she jokes ruefully to their friends that she didn't need to go through childbirth because she already has a kid in the house.

Though they do not have any degree of volatility in their fighting—there are none of the knock-down-drag-outs that characterized Rick and Dana's marriage—Mike and Nancy complain constantly about each other to just about anyone who will listen. Nancy feels that she's had to take on far more responsibility in the household than she had expected to, and Mike complains that Nancy has plenty of time for everything in her life . . . except him. As you can see, the argument is as circular as it is recurring: "You don't make time for *me!*" / "How can I make time for you when I have to spend all my time picking up the slack for the things you won't do?"

• Otto Gustafson is a very, very powerful man. Having patented three separate items that are now standard in most automobiles, he's built enormous wealth. He's also built enormous paranoia: Otto unconsciously feels like a fraud—that he's "cheated the system"—and it's a feeling he projects onto the folks around him in order to make himself feel better. He regularly accuses his relatives and coworkers of taking advantage of his kindness for their own selfish interests. No one wanders into his crosshairs more than his wife, Pauline. Neatly ignoring the fact she's been with him far longer than he's been rich—his wealth came some twenty years into their marriage—he now often berates her by saying she stays with him only so she can spend his money.

Much of the time, Pauline takes her husband's verbal abuse. She is, as she was when they married, a woman with powerful feelings of inadequacy and incompetence. She is afraid that if she sticks up for herself too strenuously, and Otto leaves her, that no one else will have her. We've seen relationships like this in earlier chapters; now we're identifying its place in the spectrum of relationships: it's a classic (and chronic) Rel-Con Three.

As we've seen in these examples—and as you'd see in any examples from your own experience that you could doubtless come up with—there are six major factors that set level three relationships apart from those on levels one and two:

1. There is an increase in the intensity and frequency of arguments and conflict.
2. Each person experiences the other's needs as excessive, inappropriate, and unreasonable.
3. Compromise isn't entered into happily; rather, it's experienced as an imposition.
4. Arguments often escalate into personal attacks . . . and the fighting can get mighty, mighty dirty.
5. Negative projective identification predominates over positive projective identification; that is, one partner (say, Otto) makes the other (say, Pauline) experience feelings (such as inadequacy) that they don't wish to recognize as their own. In a level three relationship, the need to attack and defend feels stronger than the need to nourish the union.
6. Positive feeling states, such as love, affection, and sexuality, are rarely experienced and tend to be replaced by anger, disgust, and hopelessness.

Rel-Con Four: Wait . . . Isn't There Supposed to Be Some Positive?

I have two words for you, now: *chronic* and *conflict*. Put 'em together, and you've accurately described the level four relationship. (Come to think of it, back in chapter 2, one of

Bernie's patients uttered a Freudian slip that describes the typical level four union even better: it's a "relation*shit*.") Now the strains brought on by the needs of each partner don't just stress the other's coping mechanisms, they actually threaten the other's psychological well-being.

For Sara Moss, that psychological well-being was fragile to begin with. Sara lost her father at the age of two, and her mother passed away just five years later, leaving Sara an orphan who was passed from relative to relative, none of whom were particularly interested in raising her. She describes her childhood as figuratively and literally nightmarish; Sara had such fear of the things that awaited her in her dreams that she slept with the light on well into her twenties. She grew up anxious, and was afraid to leave whatever home she was living in at the time even for short periods, for fear she wouldn't be welcomed back. (Even going to school every day filled her with anxiety.)

Sara is married to Ralph Moss, a man whose one constant psychological need is adoration. From his kids to his wife, and from his friends to his coworkers, Ralph's single demand is that he be praised in all ways and at all times. He needs to hear how superior he is, how effective he is at his job, and how good-looking he is. Ralph isn't a man of many needs, and thank goodness for that: the one he has is almost overwhelming.

And his wife is overwhelmed. When Ralph demands that Sara adore and praise him, it makes her feel alone and anxious—she told Bernie that her husband's chronic need makes her feel like she's going to be "smashed to bits by a tidal wave." In Sara's mind, Ralph's demands negate her: he's the only one that matters . . . or even exists. All of the abandonment fears she's lived with throughout her sad childhood return in full force. And so Sara tells her husband off, which only intensifies the problem, because Ralph's reaction is to first yell at his wife and then to storm off. He literally abandons her, which sends her into a psychological tailspin.

In the case of Mr. and Mrs. Moss, we get a very good picture of exactly how any attempt to meet one partner's needs can be the other partner's undoing. (Or ungluing, as it were.) Level four relationships are characterized by extraordinarily high levels of emotional pain as well as conflict. They're also characterized by a heightened cycle of blame and denial: each person accuses the other of causing all of the distress, and refuses to take responsibility for any of it. "It's all your fault!" is often heard. In addition, there's now extreme sensitivity to criticism of any kind, and a propensity to meet even innocuous statements from a partner with emotional overreaction. Couples in this sorry state frequently interrupt each other, and challenge each other's feelings and experiences.

Maybe we ought to call this the "powder keg" level, because Rel-Con Four is the romantic relationship equivalent of Def-Con One: everyone is on heightened alert, and full-scale war could break out at any time. And just about anything can set the combatants off, from a spilled glass of wine to a forgotten appointment. It doesn't really matter how trivial the subject of an argument is for a level four couple, either; it will go on for days and days, and probably involve yelling and recrimination. Which means, of course, that the typical level four argument isn't really about its stated cause, but rather the terrible feelings that each combatant is unknowingly and unwittingly inducing in the other.

In Rel-Con Four marriages, the future is always at stake: divorce is frequently threatened by one or both partners. But while many of these relationships do end in divorce, it's been Bernie's experience that a far greater number stay married, bound together for a lifetime of chronically dissatisfying, argumentative, and generally dysfunctional coupledom. To the outside world, it's inconceivable why *any* couple with so much conflict would stay together and live their lives in a constant combative stance. What supernatural power could possibly keep these people together, we wonder.

The answer, as I'll explain in a moment, is magic.

First, though, let's stroll back a few chapters and revisit the notion of idealization. You remember—that's the phase early on in a relationship, where we're projecting all of our hopes and dreams for a perfect mate onto our new partner. And while we're projecting that idealized image *onto* our partner, we're also projecting *into* our partner the warm, loving, eroticized emotions we're having as a result of our idealization. In other words, we feel good about them, and we make them feel good. It's during this phase of idealization that we feel understood, loved, cared for, and accepted. In other words, we're feeling like all of our needs are being met.

When Ralph Moss—who always needed the world to adore him—was dating Sara, she did, in fact, adore him. But not because he deserved adoration; no, Sara adored him because at the time he was the projected ideal she very much wanted and needed in her life. What she was really adoring was her own self-created fantasy of Ralph as the perfect man for her. And her good feelings radiated out of her, and were experienced by Ralph as . . . you guessed it, adoration. Since she made him feel so good, he quite naturally wanted to have her around all the time, which in turn lowered the intense separation anxiety that had plagued her since childhood.

In this positive feedback loop, Ralph and Sara each believed they had reached Nirvana; both were convinced that they had met someone perfectly suited to meet their respective needs and fulfill any deprivations from earlier experiences. As we know, this fantasy started to unravel a bit through the reality phase of their courtship. Gradually, each came to see some of the fallibilities and weaknesses the other had. But rather than accepting these disappointments and integrating them into the relationship, Ralph and Sara became increasingly angry. Rather than compromising their way through each other's more negative personality aspects, they let their conflict escalate—over time—into a level four relationship.

As couples like Ralph and Sara Moss continue a courtship and get engaged, they have arguments and bicker, but not as intensely as they will later on. That's because the commitment phase (including engagement) of a relationship still provides some distance between the partners. They're not yet completely tied emotionally, economically, legally, or socially, and so they have *just* enough distance—*just* enough idealization left over—to keep them on relatively good behavior. In other words, before marriage, couples still hold out hope for a reactivation of the good feelings they had in the early stages of the relationship, and they behave so as not to kill any chance of that reactivation.

Sometime early on in marriage, though, Ralph and Sara each recognized that the other did not have a great capacity for meeting their needs. And so their conflict began in earnest. And so did their mutual belief in magic.

The reason that couples like the Mosses often stay together for years and even decades of marital distress is that each partner grows to earnestly believe that if they can just yell loud enough or pout long enough, their spouse will magically change back into that idealized person they seemed to be early in the relationship. They are unwilling to accept the "what you see is what you get" truth of marriage, preferring to cling to the "what you *project* is what you get" fantasy left over from the attraction and idealization phases. Seriously troubled marriages grind on and on because the people in them cling to this belief: *My partner met my needs just fine when we were dating, so there must be* something *I can do to make him meet my needs once again.* Unfortunately, most folks choose to badger their spouse in the futile hope of returning to the glory days of the relationship . . . and when that badgering doesn't work, they become more and more angry. Think of it as an internal negative feedback loop: I pester them because I'm mad, and when my pestering doesn't work, I get furious.

Though couples will spend many, many years in marital distress because each partner truly believes they can get their spouse to be the person that he or she was in the early part of the relationship, the reality is that it can't happen. What we fall in love with during that early part of a relationship is a projection, an idealized version of the person that overlooks their faults and deficiencies. So it's really not the person that has changed over time and is therefore no longer meeting our needs, it's our *perception* of the person. How can we ask someone to change back into some idealized perception of what we projected onto them? There's no going back when what's behind us was never real in the first place.

There are other reasons that level four couples stay together. One is that partners use these tormented relationships as a way to work out an earlier negative family experience. In other words, people stay in long-term, conflicted relationships because in some way their spouse has become a stand-in for the parent who deprived them or frustrated them, the parent who withheld love or admiration. It's the unconscious intent of a person in such a relationship to repair and correct earlier hurts or deprivations. It's as though they can now say to their spouse all of the things that they would have liked to have said to one or both parents, but were unable to when they were younger. And as you can guess, the things they would like to have said are not pleasant.

Yet another reason that majorly conflicted couples might stay together has to do with something we looked at way back in chapter 3, the need to maintain the unconscious process of projective identification. Here's how it works, in the unconscious mind of the spouse: "I have something within my personality that I don't really want to deal with or face because it causes me a great deal of anguish. If I can project it into my partner—if I can induce him or her to actually take on that characteristic that I hate so much—then I can feel better by keeping my partner close and continually deluding myself that *they* are the one with the problem." It's a compelling reason, and Bernie has found countless couples in therapy who remain together despite horrible marital conflict solely so that each partner can maintain their psychological defenses.

Before we move away from our discussion of Rel-Con Four—and we should, soon, because it's getting depressing—let's look at two more examples of relationships that fall into this category and then summarize the features that set level four apart from the previous levels.

• Tim is an extremely volatile man. He's beset by frequent bouts of intense anxiety, and the way he copes with such episodes is by focusing his attention on his wife, Vivian. As in, he becomes completely controlling. He demands to know where she is all the time, and when she's with him, he follows her around the house, hovering over her. Vivian herself is an extremely withdrawn person. She's almost noncommunicative. For years before marrying Tim, she lived on her own, by choice.

Now she often finds herself living with a caged animal. When Tim goes through his periods of being controlling, his proximity and excessive demands push his wife even deeper into her shell, which in turn produces even more anxiety and anger in Tim. He digs in deeper. He now not only stands over his wife, he criticizes everything she's doing. Could be the way she's filing papers, or it could be the way she's loading the dishwasher; it doesn't so much matter what she's doing as long as it provides him a way to criticize her.

Eventually, in each of these bouts, Vivian will break her pattern long enough to tell her husband off, loudly. They'll fight, which will raise both of their anxiety levels through the roof. One or the other will storm off, and the separation will give them each time to let their anxieties recede back down to manageable levels. Until the next time Tim's anxiety level rises over something else, and the whole cycle starts again. The pattern of Tim's interactions with Vivian can be found on the back of just about any bottle of shampoo: lather, rinse, repeat.

• Abby, on the other hand, isn't so much controlling as she is controlled. As in, *Stepford Wives* controlled. (And by that I mean the creepy original *The Stepford Wives*—the one with Katharine Ross—and not that silly remake with Nicole Kidman.) She's a quiet, unemotional, hardworking woman who has never wanted children because she worries they'd get in the way of her career. Ask her friends what she's like, and they'll say she's pleasant enough to be around, but not exactly a barrel of laughs: there's not even a hint of spontaneity to her. When Abby feels that someone is being critical of her, she becomes defensive in a completely controlled way; that is, she intellectualizes the criticism rather than getting good and pissed off.

For her husband, Ben, control is not much of a theme in his life. Before meeting Abby, Ben had a long history of alcohol and drug abuse, though he'd managed to climb onto (and stay on) the wagon for five years before their marriage. Where his wife is reserved, Ben's personality is such that he can become demanding, angry, and accusative. When he tries to get Abby to be more emotional, she attempts to rationally explain why she isn't . . . and then goes on to criticize Ben. The things she criticizes him for are largely projections of her own issues; his often "out of control" emotional state is something she's unconsciously terrified of in herself. That is, she's a very controlled person because she's afraid of the part of her personality that wishes to be *un*controlled . . . and she projects that part of her into her husband.

It works all too well—he *is* a guy who has struggled with substance abuse, after all—and they have such nasty fights that Ben has fallen off the wagon periodically, and behaved recklessly in other ways, as well. In fact, it's amazing Ben is still alive, considering the time he drunkenly decided to punish her for saying he ought to be "locked away" by driving her treasured, meticulously kept Lexus into a local pond.

With Abby and Ben, we get a clear picture of the third reason we looked at for the longevity of level four relationships: the need to partake in a little projective identification. Abby's unconscious fear of losing control is something she projects into her husband and then berates him for. Her criticism sends him into fits of even more uncontrolled behavior, and she's able to—by staying close to him—make herself feel better by believing that he's the one with the unwanted personality trait. What's interesting in their relationship is that when their fights escalate so much that Abby finally "loses it" and explodes in anger, her ability to show even that *negative* emotion serves to calm Ben back down.

The examples we've looked at over the last several pages all contain some feature or features of a typical Rel-Con Four marriage. Here are the things that set the level four relationship apart from the ones that preceded it:

1. A psychological intolerance for a specific behavior, emotion, or way of relating that one spouse experiences as characteristic of the other spouse. This specific trait actually feels threatening to the personality and the coping mechanism of the other spouse. In the case of Mr. and Mrs. Moss, Ralph's need to be adored constantly triggered his wife's fear of rejection and abandonment. One spouse criticizes the other, in the (misguided) belief that this will bring about a personality change and a return to a better feeling state.

2. A reliance by one or both partners on negative projective identification. Ironically, in most cases the attacking spouse has an unconscious part of their own personality that is identical to the behavior they're complaining about. (In addition,

the attacker unconsciously perceives his or her spouse as the "bad parent" and may be trying to get revenge for past hurts.) As each tries to change the other, both resist, feeling they are the innocent victim of the excessive or inappropriate desires and feelings of their "misguided" spouse. What's really happening is that each is acting on an unconscious need to provoke the worst in the other. The act of inducing intense, horrible feelings through projective identifications helps each partner to:

   a. maintain a psychological balance,
   b. restore damaged or missing parts of the personality,
   c. reactivate the earlier idealizations.

3. The violation of physical and psychological boundaries becomes common and chronic. When we talk about the violation of physical boundaries, we include:

   a. Physical fighting
   b. Physical abuse
   c. Damaging a spouse's possessions
   d. Secretly siphoning money from what are supposed to be joint accounts
   e. Sexual abuse

The violation of psychological boundaries may include:

   a. intense arguments in public view, such as at family gatherings or in a restaurant.

    b. intense condemnation of the spouse's
       behavior

    c. use of violent, sexual, or derogatory
       language

    d. complaining to one's children about how
       awful one's spouse is

    e. engaging in extramarital affairs (and/or
       describing them to one's spouse)

    f. provoking intense emotional reactions in
      the spouse by attacking their greatest
      vulnerability.

4. A total unwillingness to accept any blame for the marital trouble: "It's not *my* fault!" This is created by the overwhelming need to see the spouse as "all bad," so as to not recognize the undesirable or upsetting parts of oneself.

5. A strong belief in one or both of two premises: "I can't be happy until my spouse changes," and "I can't change until my spouse does first."

6. The specter of divorce . . . but usually just the specter. In level four situations, each partner may threaten to end the marriage, but will then insist that it is the other who must initiate the separation. Ipso facto: the marriage rarely ends.

Divorce seems an awfully appropriate topic to end this chapter with, don't you think? But while we'll see it as an ending point for our discussion of the various levels of conflict in committed relationships, understand that it often isn't the end of the most severely conflicted pairings. Ironically, when one partner in a level four marriage raises the subject of splitting, the other will finally become remorseful, repentant, and forgiving. Which produces good feelings and optimism in the one threatening divorce. Such cease-fires are temporary, unfortunately. While they reduce stuff such as separation anxiety and depression, they can't stave off the underlying hostilities, and before too long, level four couples find themselves right up at the edge of the cliff all over again.

And again.

Which means it's time for us to move away from the things that cause conflicted relationships, and toward what it is we can do to start to fix them.

Four Tools for Reducing Your Rel-Con

The second syllable in Rel-Con stands for *condition,* but it might as well stand for *conflict,* because the greater the intensity of the conflict in your relationship, the higher your Rel-Con is going to go. To lower the overall stress between you and your partner, you've got to get that conflict under control. Here are four extremely useful tools that will help you do that:

1. Take a Time Out

Let's start with something so basic that it's the most common strategy used by adults who are faced with unruly children. The time out is essentially the parental version of what the referee says to boxers at the end of each round: "Break it up, and go to your corner."

There are two ways in which a time out works when it's used by a parent. First, by being sent somewhere away from the action—whether that action is a fight, a temper tantrum, or just general bad behavior—a child gets the chance to calm down and let the intensity of his or her feelings diminish. Second, that quiet space gives the kid a chance to reflect on what happened . . . and hopefully figure out how to verbalize what it is that he or she is feeling, so that the battle ends and a conversation starts.

Sounds exactly like what *you* ought to be doing when your relationship begins to feel like a war zone. If you sense a battle coming on (or even if the first few grenades have already been thrown), let your partner know you need to leave the room to calm down and think, and that you'd like to have a conversation when you're feeling more composed. It's amazing how the simple act of acknowledging that you're upset and then adding a reassurance—"I'd really like to work this out when we're both a little calmer"—can immediately reduce the tension in the room.

2. Be Your Own Play-by-Play Announcer

If you turn on your television to watch anything from a tennis match to a baseball game, chances are excellent that you're going to have every moment explained to you by the folks in the announcer's booth. TV networks pay people a ton of money to provide running commentary about every play, shot, goal, and so on, to help those of us at home understand what the athletes are attempting, and why they succeed or fail at those attempts. When you really think about it, play-by-play announcers practice the art of *observation,* and they use their knowledge of the game they're calling to put the action of the game into *perspective.*

Take a lesson from those guys and gals in the booth, and observe yourself *while* you're arguing. Think about it: how many times have you had a fight and asked yourself afterward—when it was too late to do any good—"How the heck did that get out of control?" or, worse, "What were we even arguing about?" Instead, put some very basic questions to yourself as the fight is starting and escalating: "What is it we're really arguing about?" and "Am I saying things to solve the issue at hand, or am I just trying to let my partner know how pissed off I am?" And don't ask just ask these questions of yourself; put 'em to the person you're fighting with as well. Let your partner know that your aim is to stay "on topic," and that you're trying to keep the bad feelings that come with disagreement from affecting how you argue. If you catch yourself getting really angry, or saying something just to hurt your partner, point those things out. Provide a running commentary of what you're thinking and going through. Put it into perspective: "You know, when you said _____, you really hit a nerve with me, because _____."

Self-observation, and the communication of what you're observing, is a tremendously powerful tool: it can prevent your anger from escalating and it allows you to communicate not just what you think, but also how you feel. Self-observation helps you to avoid making those attacking "you" statements—"You never . . ." "You always . . ." "You're such a . . ."—so that your partner can concentrate on solving the issue at hand, and not on playing defense. (I'll stop with the sports analogies now, I promise.)

3. Keep a Neutron Rod Handy

Here's a quick and painless lesson in nuclear science: the intensity of the energy created by a nuclear reactor—and the potential for a disastrous explosion—is controlled by a little something called a neutron rod. Insert such a rod into a reactor, and the rod's literal powers of attraction cause the neutrons in the reactor to become attached to it, thereby lowering the intensity of the energy the reactor produces. Pull the neutron rod out, and the neutrons start running free again, producing the energy for a potential nuclear reaction.

Think of your relationship as a nuclear reactor—after some fights, it's hard *not* to think of it that way—and figure out what might act as a neutron rod, should the energy of an argument start to get out of hand. For your purposes, a neutron rod is anything that can reliably calm your partner down. Maybe that's simply *telling* them they need to calm down; maybe it's acknowledging how upset they clearly are. Maybe it's giving them a compliment or asking them to explain what they're feeling at that exact moment. You know what? It could even be something as little as telling them a joke: use your knowledge of your partner to find the right tension-reducer that works for them.

> Think of your relationship as a nuclear reactor—after some fights, it's hard *not* to think of it that way—and figure out what might act as a neutron rod, should the energy of an argument start to get out of hand.

And whatever it is, *do it*, even though you probably won't much feel like it. (I mean, who wants to give a compliment to someone whose head they'd like to remove?) Remember, the object is to control the "energy" of the argument; anything you can do to reduce the risk of explosion will only make your life easier—and your relationship healthier—in the long run.

4. Acknowledgize

It's tempting, in the heat of battle, to say some version of the following to your partner: "This is all *your* fault." But you know what? It isn't. It takes two to argue, and chances are pretty good—okay, extremely good—that if you take a hard look at the things that have been said back and forth during a fight, there's plenty of blame to share. Silently acknowledging your own role in a fight has a positive, calming effect: when you turn a bit of the blame for the fight inward, your anger decreases, and your ability to be reasonable increases.

> It's tempting, in the heat of battle, to say some version of the following to your partner: "This is all your fault."

So why not share the wealth? Here's a novel idea: verbally *acknowledge* your role in the escalation of the fight, and then go a step further and *apologize* for it, on the spot. "Look, this is getting out of hand, and I know I've said things to upset you . . . and I'm sorry for saying those things." Or, "We're both pretty clearly angry, and I want you to know that making you angry makes me feel terrible, so I'd like to apologize for whatever it is that I've done to upset you." One other great way to *acknowledgize* is to say some version of the following: "You know, you just made a really good point, and I'm sorry I didn't see it sooner."

You can always follow any one of these statements with, "It's important to me that we figure this problem out, but it's even more important that you realize I don't want to hurt you." You can even ask your partner to let you know when they think you've gone over the line. When you stop a fight long enough to "acknowledgize," you're giving yourself and your partner a chance to stop focusing on the *fight* and start looking at the *problem.*

6

Getting What You Want . . . and Wanting What You've Got

Forewarned, as they say, is forearmed. The problem is, most folks entering into a committed relationship wouldn't recognize a warning sign if it came tattooed on a new lover's backside. Oh, sure: years *later,* we're able to look back and list the things that should have given us pause . . . but how were we supposed to see them early on, when our idealization of our partner was in full swing? This is the common lament of people in marriage counseling: "Sure, we had arguments—who doesn't?—but since we always managed to get through them, we never thought they'd get out of hand. Living with someone is supposed to get *easier* over time, not harder."

You have to say this about romantic love: it may be naive, but it sure is *hopeful.*

As we've seen in earlier chapters, the conflicts that couples face early on don't dissipate as a result of marriage; instead, they tend to escalate. Which means it's vital to recognize potential problems early in a relationship—or, if it's too late for that, to understand why our long-term relationships have the chronic problems that they do—and to develop strategies for handling conflict so as to minimize the stress it puts on us *and* on our partners. The first step toward assessing and improving a relationship, then, is to observe the relationship as it is progressing (or to think back upon its progression) with an eye toward understanding the role of each person in that relationship. To do this, we're going to follow three simple rules:

Know Thyself
Know the Other
and
Know the Process

Know Thyself

The term *Know Thyself* implies that each of us has some ability to self-observe. And most of us do: with any reasonable level of emotional maturity, it's quite possible to take a step back from just about any situation and observe it as it unfolds. That is, to experience that situation externally—to do and say the things we think we should—while at the same time recognizing our internal reactions, which may be very different from what we show the outside world. Think of it this way:

I'm going to guess you've been on blind dates. Most of us

have been fixed up by friends at least once in our lives, and many of us more than once. So chances are good you know the exquisite tension of ringing a doorbell (or waiting for your doorbell to ring) and then having the door opened to . . . someone you never would have chosen to go out with. And how do you react? If you have any tact at all, you externally react with enthusiasm: "Hi! I'm so happy to meet you," or "You look terrific!" Internally, of course, there's a whole other thing going on: "I will *kill* my friend for fixing me up with this person," or "Hmm . . . is there a place we can go for dinner where there's no chance that anyone I know will see us together?" Self-observation, then, is simply an awareness of our internal reactions to things, regardless of what our external reactions are.

Self-observation is a process that operates in every interpersonal situation. Think of a job interview: inside, you may be thinking "Wow, he *hates* me," or "How does she want me to answer this question?" or even "I wish I was coming off a little hungrier, and not so self-assured." But the stuff you're showing your interviewer is completely different. You're smiling, talking enthusiastically, and working very hard to keep your nervousness under wraps. What you're really doing, of course, is putting your self-observation to immediate use: based on your private, internal reactions to the interviewer, you're constantly modifying your behavior and honing your responses so as to maximize your chances of getting the job.

So let's amend that definition of self-awareness from a few paragraphs back: it isn't simply the act of observing your internal reactions, it's also a device that allows you to be introspective, to increase your self-awareness, and to monitor that complex world inside your own psyche. It is an essential piece of your personality structure. If you think about it, the opposite of self-observation are two little devices known as denial and repression, the processes we use when we want to obscure the way we're feeling by pushing away any internal reaction that's too negative, unpleasurable, or anxiety-producing.

There's a constant internal battle between our capacity for self-awareness and our capacity for suppression when we're faced with difficult life choices and situations. Say, for example, you're out on a date with someone who happens to be really attractive . . . and yet you find yourself having inexplicable pangs of boredom. Your first instinct is probably to try to ignore the boredom so as not to blow your chances with the hottie across the table. Well, not so fast: if you're practicing self-observation, you will not only allow yourself to experience the boredom, you'll go a step further and try to figure out the cause of that boredom. You'll see your feeling of boredom not as an impediment, but rather as a warning sign: "Maybe I'm bored because this person bores me, or is irritating me in some way, or is way too self-absorbed."

The trick is not to discard (or repress) the valuable information that self-observation digs up. Knowing yourself takes effort, a keen mental eye, and a willingness to honestly confront the things that cause you distress. It takes self-observation, and it also takes self-reflection. To know yourself in relation to your romantic experiences and history, you need to self-observe and you need to be able to sit in a room, alone with your thoughts . . . and that journal we've talked about. It's there that you should ask yourself a series of questions, and see how many of them you can jot down answers to:

1. What kind of person do I typically get romantically involved with?
   a. What are their characteristics?
   b. What are their behavior patterns?
   c. What are their physical characteristics . . . do I have a "type"?
2. Why do my relationships end?
   a. Am I the one who usually initiates breakups?
   b. Do other people usually break up with me?
   c. Do I tend to lose interest quickly?
   d. Are there any chronic conflicts that affect most of my relationships?
   e. How long do my relationships usually last?
   f. Does being in a relationship usually result in my feeling anxious, bored, or depressed?
3. What are my good and bad points when it comes to being in a relationship?
   a. Would my lovers say I'm a giver or a taker?
   b. Do I tend to be more, less, or equally as affectionate as the person I'm involved with?
   c. Am I communicative?
   d. Do I withdraw emotionally . . . and if so, what precipitates my withdrawal?
   e. Do I get angry or upset easily?
   f. Do I do things for the other person . . . and then resent them for letting me do them?
4. How well do I know the impact of my family on me?
   a. How did my parents get along with each other?

b. How would I characterize the relative success or failure of their marriage?
c. How did I relate to each of them?
d. How am I like each of them?
e. What was my role in the family, and are there ways in which I'm now somehow re-creating that role in my romantic relationships?

Don't stop with those, of course. Try to think about the factors and forces that shaped your personality, and consider how they might be affecting your relationship. Considering the role your personality plays in the ultimate success or failure of any romantic bond you might enter into, it makes sense to look as deeply into yourself as you're able.

Which is hard work, I know. (Believe me, I know: just ask six or seven of my old girlfriends. Self-reflection was something that came to me a little later in life than I'd have liked.) It's never easy to look at yourself, because we all tend to deny or repress painful feelings and experiences. If you find yourself struggling with questions such as the ones above—if you're searching for answers that seem to have left your memory banks for the safer haven of your unconscious—there is another way of collecting self-data. Namely, asking people. Find friends that you've had since

> There is another way of collecting self-data. Namely, asking people. Find friends that you've had since childhood, and ask them to tell you what they know about you.

childhood, and ask them to tell you what they know about you. Look up an old girlfriend or boyfriend or two—or *six*—and ask them (nicely) the questions about yourself that you can't answer. Ask them for their impression of why you broke up. (And accept their answers graciously. Remember: you asked!) If you can find a relative who will be honest with you, go ahead and ask them about your childhood.

(Author's note: I'd like to officially apologize to that former boss that I ridiculed in the introduction, the one who handed me the business school exercise aimed at improving self-knowledge. Clearly, finding out what other people know about you that you don't know about yourself is important and tremendously helpful. Sorry, boss. You may have been pompous, sexist, and cruel—hey, just helping you with your self-knowledge, here—but you were right about this one. My bad.)

What you'll find fascinating when you look at your notes—and probably a little frightening—is how often other peoples' perceptions of you will be at odds with your own self-perceptions. Bernie has a patient who considers himself to be a free-thinking, highly independent, self-motivated guy . . . who somehow manages to constantly find himself taking the backseat in his romantic relationships. In his love affairs, he plays a very passive role, permitting and even encouraging his girlfriends to take the lead and direct the course of the relationship. Shortly after Bernie convinced him that a little self-fact-finding might be in order, he was shocked and upset to learn—during a conversation with an old school buddy—that when he was growing up his parents always told him what to do and how to do it. He had always gone along with their wishes and instructions, and yet developed the illusion over time that he had been the one making decisions.

Finding that honest relative to talk to, as I said a few paragraphs back, might be a challenge. People that you're related to might well be a lot less objective, for fear of offending you or someone else that they're (also) related to. It's kind of hard to get your aunt to tell you unflattering things about your similarities to your father . . . because she'll still have to see you and your father at family gatherings, you know? But try: relatives can be major resources in attempting to gather self-information.

Once you've gathered that information, through self-reflection and/or from others who were in a position to observe your personality and its traits develop, read through it and look for patterns. See what's consistent and corroborated. That's the stuff that probably permeated your earlier relationships, and flows through the one you may currently be in. That's the stuff that shapes the romantic events in your life.

> You're going to have to make some room for your brain when it comes to all things romantic, and gently tell your heart that it can't run the whole show.

Now, here's the $64,000 question: given all this new knowledge about yourself, can you change in ways that will improve your romantic relationship? The answer is *yes* . . . if you're willing to do the work. You'll have to first develop an awareness of the content of your personality, and then you'll have to exert a little informed, intellectual control over your emotions. In other words, you're going to have to make some room for your brain when it comes to all things romantic, and gently tell your heart that it can't run the whole show. You're going to have to learn to find the balance between what your heart wants, and what your head knows . . . and then you're going to have to live with that balance, and the compromises that it necessitates.

As Joe Daniels learned the hard way.

Joe had a habit, from his college days on, of falling in love intensely . . . and frequently. Almost instantaneously, Joe could develop strong loving and erotic feelings for women he'd just met. He'd sweep them off their feet, and then almost as quickly, he'd lose interest and disappear. Until the day he met Lynne. Oh, he fell for her just as hard and as fast, but this time he got married. And that marriage was terrific. For about a month and a half. After just three months as man and wife, Joe and Lynne separated. Devastated by his failure to stay interested in his wife, Joe began therapy.

Those women that he'd fall for? As he discovered through guided self-reflection, they all had one trait in common. Actually, three: all of them, including Lynne, turned out to be cold, emotionally ungiving, and self-centered. Which, oddly enough, is exactly how Joe described his mother to his therapist.

What Joe came to realize is that the intense feelings he would instantly experience with a new girlfriend could not be trusted. In fact, they were a terrific indication that any long-term relationship with that woman would be doomed. While they felt *good,* and on the surface seemed positive, Joe's surges of erotic, romantic feelings were more of a danger sign than anything else. And so he learned to heed the warnings. Joe is now remarried, quite happily, to a woman who gives him a great deal of love, support, satisfaction, and pleasure, but to whom he was not initially attracted. Sometimes, he laments that he never experienced intense feelings for his current wife . . . but he knows that if he did, she'd probably end up as the *second* ex-Mrs. Daniels.

So change *is* possible, given self-knowledge, self-reflection, and a willingness to compromise. For Joe, change—and a more rewarding relationship—came when he understood that his pattern of romantic behavior was maladaptive; that his intense feelings toward certain women were related to his very early bonding with a cold, distant mother. Even though the feelings his pattern brought him were wonderful, they always led to relationship hell. As Joe so ably demonstrates, *Know Thyself* is the first step in breaking a self-destructive romantic pattern.

Know the Other

Repression isn't always something we do with our own stuff; sometimes we're more than willing to push the things we know about a new partner's personality out of our mind, so we can avoid the unpleasantness of doubting whether that person is romantically right for us. While that's an understandable impulse, it's also a dumb one: seeing a partner's personality and patterns of behavior as clearly as possible is *critical* to making informed decisions about the course of a relationship. In other words, you ignore warning signs at your own peril.

To *Know the Other*—the person you're romantically involved with—is once again a matter of data collection. Since self-reflection won't help here, and you really can't pry into a partner's life by asking their friends and relatives for the inside scoop on their childhood, your options are . . . well, there's really only one option: talk to your partner. (But this time, leave your journal in a drawer. This is their stuff, not yours.) Ask questions about their past relationships. We'll take a look at what to say if your questions make them bristle in just a moment. Try to understand why those relationships ended. And don't accept the typical intellectualized or superficial answers they might give you to try to justify and explain why a particular relationship ended; be wary of statements like these:

"We simply outgrew each other."
"We fell out of love."
"We realized we didn't have much in common."
"I guess I just wasn't ready for a commitment."

When people say these kinds of things, what they're really saying is that they'd rather avoid facing some very powerful issues having to deal with their own unconscious and/or their ability to function in a relationship. *Which is exactly why you're asking in the first place: you're trying to recognize and attempting to deal with these issues before they sabotage your relationship.*

To avoid getting only pat answers to your questions, the trick is to ask a bunch of specific questions that are all designed to get at the same basic theme about each of your partner's significant past relationships: "What went on between the two of you that ultimately led one or both of you to end the relationship?" Here are some examples of questions you might ask:

- What were your complaints about your partner?
- What did you tend to argue about?
- When you had differences of opinion, what were they about?
- What did your friends think of your partner?
- What habits did your partner have that made you crazy?
- What kinds of negative feelings did your partner produce in you?

Oh, and while you're asking relationship questions, make sure you get in this one, which is general, but oh, so important:

- How long have your past relationships tended to last?

When you start asking a partner about their romantic history, you might very well get one of the following reactions: "I can't see how that stuff is any of your business," or "You sound just like a shrink." You might be intimidated by either of these responses—which would make sense, because these responses are meant to intimidate you into withdrawing your questions—and you might be tempted to apologize. Don't. Instead, explain that you're simply trying to make the relationship as strong as possible. Is their history your business?

You bet it is: as we've talked about, romantic behavior tends to be repetitive, so your lover's past relationships are an important prologue to the one you're currently having with them. (In other words, whatever they did to former lovers, they'll do to you.) And, to be fair, your past relationships are *their* business, so offer up the same information about your past that you're asking them for.

If they make the shrink comment, here's an easy way to handle it: "I guess maybe I *do* sound like a shrink. From what I know about shrinks, they gather information in order to make an intelligent assessment of what a person is like. It's really important to me to know what you're like, so I'm just asking for information. Is there anything you'd like to know about me?" It's hard to argue with someone who takes a cheap shot like "You sound just like a shrink" and gives it a thoughtful response.

What you're looking for, of course, when your partner tells you about past relationships, is some idea of your partner's behavior patterns and emotional hot buttons: these are the things you're most likely to face as your relationship progresses. And then again, maybe you won't. Maybe *this* relationship will actually be completely different for them than any relationship in the past . . . which is a lovely thought, but not likely. So why take a chance? *Know the Other.* Gather information.

And be very honest with your partner about why you're gathering information. Tell them that you'd like to know what their issues have been historically (and you'd like them to know about your past relationship issues), because those are the things that are most likely to recur in your committed relationship or marriage. Those are the potential trouble areas. What you're really saying, of course, is something tremendously flattering to them: "I'm invested in this relationship and I want to do whatever I can to make it run as smoothly as possible. I really believe it's wise to talk about the potentially difficult stuff early on, rather than let that stuff grow unchecked and maybe injure this relationship that means so much to me." Wouldn't *you* like to hear that from your partner?

(It's quite possible that you read the last paragraph and thought, "Swell . . . but I've been married for sixteen *years,* so it's a little late in the game for that kind of a chat with my spouse." Actually, it isn't. You can gather information at any point; all that changes is the way you present your desire to do so to your partner: "You know, it's so upsetting to me when we fight, and I think that maybe if we looked at some of our arguments—and maybe the way we got along with the people we were each with before we were lucky enough to find each other—we might get a few clues as to *why* we fight the way we do.")

Straight talk isn't just for preventative maintenance, though: it's perfectly acceptable—and really, really smart—to bring up painful thoughts or feelings at any point in a relationship, from the early phases all the way through the fiftieth wedding anniversary and beyond. Think of it this way: an unpleasant conversation beats the hell out of a relationship-sabotaging action, like adultery or abandonment. If one partner in a relationship or marriage is miserable and contemplating something drastic (like adultery or abandonment), it's much better for that person to sit down with their spouse and say something like, "I'm really unhappy in our relationship and

I'm wondering if I'd be better off with someone else," than to just go out and *find* someone else. Talking about such extreme feelings isn't going to make either party feel great, but it just might bring about a conversation or an action that can begin to fix the cause of the unhappiness. Communication is a critical, and potentially magical, thing: it can save your relationship, if you give it a chance.

In your effort to *Know the Other,* asking the right questions of him or her is important, but it's not enough. It's also tremendously helpful to observe their parents and siblings, and to observe your partner interact with those parents and siblings. Then see if you can answer the same kinds of questions that you've already asked of (and about) yourself: how do my partner's parents get along? How do each of them relate to my partner? What are the marriages of my partner's siblings like? Very often, it's possible to see different patterns of family relating when you watch the brothers and sisters of your partner, and see whether or not their romantic relationships are conflicted, satisfying, argumentative, happy, and so on. Here's hoping that when you do get a chance to see your partner's siblings' relationships in action, what you observe is loving and supportive behavior. If that's the case, it bodes really well for the probability of satisfaction in a long-term relationship with your partner.

Know the Process

As we've seen, romantic relationships run a very specific course: they start with attraction, and then work their way through idealization, reality, commitment, and ultimately marriage. It's important to keep in mind that when you're in a relationship, your feelings and responses to your partner are influenced by the natural course of development of that relationship. In other words, how you feel depends upon how far along you are.

In a lot of ways, the growth of a relationship is similar to the growth of a person within the context of his or her family of origin. We all start life seeing our parents as powerful, all-giving, omnipotent people. We're sure, at first, that they have all the knowledge, strength, and resources we will ever need. Ah, but then we grow up, and develop the intelligence and perception that will enable us to do some serious damage to that "omnipotent parent" illusion. We start to see the fallibilities and weaknesses that our parents possess. As a result, we feel disappointed and upset. Ultimately, we have to accept our parents for who they are; we have to come to terms with the fact that they aren't perfect people.

We also have to face up to the fact that we aren't so perfect, either. Because personalities are forged from internalized experience, our personalities contain aspects of our parents' personalities, and those aspects are good and . . . not so good. Those aspects—the building blocks of our personalities—are both conscious and unconscious, so we're not always able to anticipate our own reactions to people and situations. Which makes an interesting recipe for relationship stew, when you think about it:

Empty several cups of your own good/bad, conscious/unconscious personality traits, along with several cups of a partner's good/bad, conscious/unconscious personality traits into one large frying pan (henceforth known as "the relationship"). Stir the mixture slowly but steadily throughout the attraction/idealization/reality/commitment/marriage phases, or until done. Serves two.

Okay, I'm goofing, but it's not a completely bad analogy: the ingredients of your respective personalities are not always going to complement each other, so the best way to end up with a relationship stew that doesn't taste terrible is to know as much as you can about those ingredients, so you can futz with the seasoning as you go. *Know the Process* means "understand how the phases of a relationship interact with your personality traits, and those of your partner . . . because that interaction will determine the success (or failure) of your relationship."

Which brings us back to that analogy between a romantic relationship and early childhood bonding with a parent. Adult relationships, too, progress from idealization—in this case there's a "perfect partner" instead of a "perfect parent"—to the reality phase, where we come to see the liabilities of the other person, and not just their assets. Eventually, we make peace with the idea that the other person has good qualities as well as bad qualities, and we make sacrifices and compromises in order to produce a mutually gratifying relationship . . . just as we did (or tried to do) with our folks. Here's the big difference between our developing relationship with our parents and the one we experience with a romantic partner: our childhood relationship shapes our personality, and our adult romantic relationship is shaped *by* our personality. Actually, there's another big difference: by the time we're ready for a committed romantic relationship, we have enough intelligence and awareness to observe the process. This time around, we can help the relationship along by gathering information and forming an understanding of our self, our partner, *and* the process.

Let's take a moment to play a round of forensic psychologist, shall we? (Call this exercise *DSI: Divorce Scene Investigation,* if you like.) We'll look at the case history of Chuck and Diane, and see if we can put what we've learned so far to use in trying to figure out why their relationship failed.

The facts:

- Both Chuck and Diane had been divorced for several years when they met on a blind date. Immediately attracted to each other, they dated frequently, got engaged in record time, and were married four months after their first date.
- Before the wedding, Chuck noted several angry outbursts on the part of Diane. Since those outbursts were always short-lived, and since Diane always apologized soon after, both chose to let her pattern of outburst/remorse go unremarked upon.
- Right after the wedding, Diane's pattern got worse: her attacks escalated in intensity and frequency, and her apologies became more halfhearted and eventually stopped. And so did the marriage: just six months

after saying their vows, Chuck and Diane filed for legal separation.

As you no doubt spotted right away, Chuck and Diane made two major, major mistakes. First, they went straight from idealization to marriage: they were so impulsively wed that their relationship had no time to go through the critical phases of *reality* and *commitment*. The second mistake came in their handling—or, rather, their nonhandling—of Diane's premarital outbursts. Both should have recognized those outbursts as a warning of future trouble, and both should have looked hard for the root causes of Diane's bouts of anger. For Chuck, that would have involved asking his wife-to-be a series of questions about her past experiences with anger, especially in her previous marriage. For Diane, dealing with her own anger issues would have involved some self-observation coupled with a bit of honest self-reflection.

Even our quick *DSI* investigation offers ample proof that Chuck and Diane broke all three of the rules we've just been looking at. Each blew the chance to *Know Thyself,* because they each refused to be even mildly self-reflective—Diane about her outbursts and Chuck about his clear need to suppress any distress over those outbursts. By the same token, neither made any effort to *Know the Other.* But then, with a courtship that didn't even last as long as the typical professional sports season, how could they have learned much? Finally, their mutual head-in-the-sand, hurry-up-and-marry approach to their relationship gave Chuck and Diane virtually no chance to *Know the Process.* If they'd spent the time to get to know each other (and themselves), and then made the effort to understand how the process of building a romantic relationship can dictate and affect each partner's behavior, they might have been able to foresee the conflict that characterized their brief marriage. They might have had some chance to shift the conflicted/gratifying balance of their relationship to their favor.

As Strother Martin said so memorably to Paul Newman in the classic movie *Cool Hand Luke,* what we have here is a failure to communicate. For Chuck and Diane, an honest attempt at talking through their issues could have spared them a world of trouble. Perhaps they'd have parted ways sooner, and not rushed into a marriage. Perhaps they still would have married, but with a far more realistic picture of what that marriage would be like. No matter what the outcome of honest, constructive conversation, it would have been better than their near-instantaneous divorce. The most important tool in any relationship, in fact, the one tool that is a critical part of following our three rules—*Know Thyself, Know the Other,* and *Know the Process*—is effective, well-maintained communication.

7.

Katz's Rules
of Engagement

Communication, according to Mr. Webster, is "a process by which information is exchanged between individuals." In other words, it's an *interpersonal* process, a way of relating. When we talk about communication, we usually mean with words, but we actually do it in all kinds of ways; we communicate with gestures, with the tone of our voice, and with our actions. (As my friend likes to say to her husband, each time he promises to be less of a schmuck, "actions speak louder than words.") For communication between romantic partners to be effective, it has to be a two-way street—each has to take turns being an imparter and a receiver of information.

As relationships evolve from the early phase of idealization through the later phases of commitment and marriage, communication is an active part of the process. Though we don't really stop to consider the effect our words might have on people in the course of normal daily life, *anyone* who's ever been in a relationship can attest to the awesome power words have to produce the full spectrum of emotions in a partner. The simple act of talking can make us feel close and intimate, and it can also create anger and distance.

Of course, we only tend to think of "having a talk" with our partner in a negative sense: nobody says "we need to talk" when things are peachy in their relationship, they say it when something problematic has to be addressed. Which makes attempts at communicating with a partner a little scary. If we're raising a subject, or "having a talk," it must mean there's a problem . . . which just about guarantees we'll both be on guard and defensive, because feelings are on the line. (Our feelings, *and* our partner's.) Not a great starting point for a conversation, huh?

Actually, that's a matter of perspective.

Let's take a moment to retrain our brains in terms of how we view the act (and the art) of communication with our romantic partner. Let's understand that a conversation doesn't *bring with it* bad or unpleasant feelings—those already exist if we feel the need to "have a talk"—but is instead the only way we might be able to resolve whatever conflict we're faced with, so that we can go back to having *good* feelings. Conversation, properly understood, is a road—okay, *the* road—to positive change. The trick is to have a map, an understanding of how to navigate around the bumps and potholes in that road.

> Conversation, properly understood, is a road—okay, *the* road—to positive change.

Couples that get into the same fights over and over again serve as classic examples of failed communication. They're the folks who've forgotten (or never understood) that communication is an *interpersonal process*—it takes two to talk—in which the *way* information is passed back and forth is just as important as the information itself. Good feelings are possible through conversation only when both people in that conversation come away from it feeling *heard* and *understood*. Though it may seem daunting, this idea of navigating through conversations that may include hurt and angry feelings is actually quite possible to do . . . provided you follow four basic rules of the road:

Rule #1: Listen Up
Rule #2: Validate (Don't Negate)
Rule #3: Keep Your Cool
and
Rule #4: Mind the Gap

Just about every gym teacher I ever had—and a few over-caffeinated academic teachers, as well—had a particular fondness for the phrase "Listen up, people!" Listening up wasn't just listening; as a command, it meant "stop whatever you're doing and turn your full focus and attention on me, right now." It meant, "What I am about to tell you is important, and you better hear it." In gym class, of course, this was usually an overstatement: the announcement that we'd all have to get our permission slips signed for track tryouts wasn't usually earth-shattering. It would have sufficed had Coach Thompson dropped the second word, and simply asked us all to "listen."

In communicating with a partner, however, it *isn't* enough to just listen: you really do have to *Listen Up*. Words are a way for one person to convey an inner experience to another, especially in the context of a romantic relationship. We tell our partners not just what we want or what we're thinking, but also how we *feel*. And when we do that, when we allow our lover or spouse access into our most private stuff, we expect them to be receptive and attentive. If you come home and say, "*Man,* did I have a stressful day at work," what you want to hear in response is some version of, "That's terrible . . . what happened?" What you don't want to hear is, "You think *you* had a bad day? Well, let me tell you what *I* had to deal with," or "All you ever do is complain," or "Could you pass the salt?" Listening up is the act of attending to the other person: allowing them to communicate their experience, thoughts, or feelings.

If you think about it, your ability to really listen to someone grows in relation to your interest in what they have to say. Certain situations demand complete attention: if Scarlett Johansson were to call me up and say, "You know what trait I find sexiest in a forty-three-year-old man?" I would be rendered completely incapable of doing anything *except* listening to the next thing she had to say. (And then, a month or so later, I suspect I'd have to pay almost as much attention to my wife's attorney.) If the rich old guy down the street saw you one day and said, "You know, I actually buried a few million bucks out in the woods, and here's how to find it," you'd probably manage to turn your iPod off and focus on his next words. The more interested we are in what someone is saying, the better we listen.

To help yourself *Listen Up,* start by realizing that you're really helping *yourself* when you pay close attention to what your partner has to say: understanding their feelings today can save you from all kinds of fighting and grief tomorrow. We've talked about projective identification enough to know that you each have the power to make the other feel happy/sad/enraged/and so forth, and that those feelings tend to be passed back and forth between you. Making your partner feel listened to will very likely also make them happy . . . and if not, you'll at least alleviate some of their *un*happiness. Which means by listening, you're increasing your chances of having good stuff projected back in your direction.

Here's how to *Listen Up,* in three easy steps: first, *know your cue.* There are certain phrases or words that can reliably tip you off when it's time to listen. "Feel" is the big one, as in "I feel . . ." or "You make me feel . . ." Obviously, the phrase "we need to talk" is a giant flashing neon sign that you need to attend to your partner. Over time, you'll learn what things your partner is likely to say when he or she has something of consequence to tell you. Those words should trigger our second easy step, which is *drop what you're doing.* Log off that computer, shut down the television, put away your magazine, and put your focus completely on your partner. Turn toward them, and uncross your arms and legs: show them the "I'm paying attention, and I'm open to what you have to say" body language. Finally, *hold your tongue.* Okay, maybe this isn't the

> The phrase "we need to talk" is a giant flashing neon sign that you need to attend to your partner.

easiest step in the world, because you'll want to interrupt a dozen times, to defend yourself, or clarify things, or tell them that they're being crazy/stupid/unfair/whatever. Don't. This is your partner's time to let you know what they think and how they feel. We'll get to how you can and should respond in a bit, but for now, just *Listen Up*.

Sometimes the things you'll be listening to will be criticisms . . . of you. The rule remains in place, though: your job as a listener is to absorb what's being said, to ask for clarification when you need it, and to focus your attention on every form of communication your partner is using; pay attention to how they're saying what they're saying, and any other nonverbal cues that they may be giving. (For instance, if their arms and legs are crossed in full-on defensive posture—the way I just told you yours *shouldn't* be—recognize that they're nonverbally *screaming* "I'm feeling angry!") Your chance to respond to the criticism will come soon enough, and keep this in mind: if you're constructive in your listening—if you let your partner have their say—you'll already have diffused some of their negative emotion. You'll already have taken the first step toward genuine, productive conflict resolution.

Here's the thicket in which all too many attempts at communication between partners get lost: the distinction between *listening* and *accepting*. For many folks, hearing something with which they don't agree is almost physically painful, and to stave off that pain, they need to reject what they're hearing. They need to negate it. Here's a silly example: I once dated a woman who could not be disagreed with about *anything*. I'd offer up a positive opinion of a movie we'd just seen, and she'd become outraged. "How could you *like* that? The plot was stupid and the acting was terrible. There wasn't one good thing about that whole movie. I can't believe you say you liked it." She did the same thing about the Italian hero sandwiches I used to order from a sub shop every Sunday. Prosciutto, mozzarella, roasted red peppers: basically heaven on a roll, with oil and vinegar. They were a treat to myself, and even though I never suggested she should so much as take a bite of one, every Sunday she sang the same song: "That's *disgusting!* How could you put that in your mouth? Ecch . . . I would never eat that crap." (You know, those sandwiches tasted even better after we broke up.)

You don't have to accept the stuff that a partner says. You don't have to agree with their thoughts or opinions. You don't even have to understand their feelings. What you *do* have to do is *Validate (Don't Negate)*. When you validate what a partner is saying to you, you're acknowledging and understanding that they have every right to think and feel the way they do. Arguments between romantic partners can become intense and prolonged when either of the partners disallows the experiences or feelings of the other through negation. Bernie hears this all the time in marital therapy sessions: "Well, *I* would never feel that way." His response is, "That may very well be true. *For you.* But

> You don't have to accept the stuff that a partner says. You don't have to agree with their thoughts or opinions. You don't even have to understand their feelings.

your spouse has these feelings, and that's what we're talking about now."

Not long ago, one of Bernie's patients was trying to impress upon her husband that she is terrified of flying and experiences almost overwhelming anxiety every time she steps onto a plane. "She's just being silly," her husband told Bernie, right in front of her. "Everyone knows that statistically speaking, she's taking a far greater risk driving on the Long Island Expressway. Flying is perfectly safe." Though his response sounded almost reasonable—though a bit condescending—it infuriated his wife. "Why can't he simply acknowledge that I'm afraid?" she asked Bernie, clearly exasperated.

When you validate your partner's experience, thoughts, or feelings, you make them feel three very good things: acknowledged, heard, and understood. These are the feelings that help maintain the good stuff within a relationship. These are the feelings that cause a person to feel positively toward their partner. Now, considering this, you'd think that we'd fall all over ourselves to validate just about anything our partner says, 24/7 . . . I mean, why wouldn't we just naturally want to do something that gets such great results?

Because it's hard, that's why. It's one thing to validate someone's taste in take-out food, or to make a spouse feel understood when they express a fear of flying. It's quite another when what you're being asked to validate is something unflattering about *you*. It's hard to sit quietly—or to say accepting things—when you're being criticized, or when you're being told that your actions are causing your partner some distress. No one likes hearing complaints about themselves. So you negate, instead of validate. You reject. Here's what happens: upon getting a message from a partner that you find negative toward you, you feel as though your self-esteem is being damaged. You feel attacked. That brings about an emotional reaction in you that can range from hurt and anger all the way to frustration and rage. Most likely, you feel a desire to be critical right back, or to deny the accusation. In the attempt to protect—or somehow restore—yourself, you end up either damaging or completely shutting down the communication.

Don't think I was picking on you when I used the pronoun "you" in the last paragraph. Most of us handle criticism the same way. With anger, and negation. *It isn't true* and *how dare you* are probably the two most often heard responses when partners criticize each other. What ought to be heard, and what you might try to practice, is a phrase that's hard to say, but can mean the difference between pointless battle and productive communication: "Thank you for letting me know how you feel."

A few years back, I was skiing with a friend when I accidentally cut off a snowboarder who was trying to keep up enough speed to make it through a flat part of the ski run. The guy managed to avoid me, but still totally cussed me out as he went by, and I was furious. I caught up to my friend, told him what had happened, and he assured me that the unwritten rules of skiing were with me: since I was ahead of the snowboarder, it was his job to get around me, not my job to keep out of his way. "Still," he said, "it *is* sort of common courtesy, in that particular spot, to give snowboarders the right of way." We skied on, I calmed down, and eventually reached the bottom. Where the snowboarder was waiting for me, still clearly pissed off.

I think that if he'd surprised me, or snuck up on me, the confrontation might have gone differently. But I had a bit of time as I took off my skis to think about how to handle the guy. I chose—though I certainly didn't know the psychological term for it at the time—validation.

"What the hell is wrong with you?" he started, and I held up my hand, which shushed him.

"You're absolutely right for being pissed," I said. "I should have been aware of anyone behind me, trying to get through the flat." He sputtered, stunned that his aggression wasn't met with the same. I went on. "I just started skiing about a year ago, and I'm just not that good yet . . . with either the skis *or* the manners." The guy calmed down right before my eyes, and nodded his head. "It's cool," he said. "Just be careful in those spots, 'cause you can get *flattened.*" He'd gone from wanting to punch me to giving me pointers. Oh, and then he told me that he'd watched me come down the last part of the run, which was pretty steep, and that I actually had good form for someone who was new to the sport. As Bernie tells his patients all the time, nondefensive, validating responses can have an enormous impact on the nature of the relationship. As in, I validated the guy, and his fist *didn't* make an enormous impact on my face.

> As Bernie tells his patients all the time, nondefensive, validating responses can have an enormous impact on the nature of the relationship.

It's all too easy, when you're feeling criticized or attacked, to keep your self-esteem intact by attacking right back, or by demeaning your accuser. "What's wrong with you?" and "You're an idiot," and "You have absolutely no idea of what you're talking about," are all classic ways to defend your own righteousness. Unfortunately, they're also effective ways to cut off the conversation . . . which, even though you're mad, is not what you want to do. Cutting off the conversation won't help you to deal with the criticism and whatever may or may not be causing it. Though it's perfectly normal to feel angry and demeaned, and to want to say angry and demeaning things right back, it's counterproductive: to fix problems and return to a good feeling state, you have to keep communicating.

So *Keep Your Cool.* Take a breath. Think about what you want to say, and then ask yourself this: is what I'm going to say designed to move the conversation forward, or is it meant to hurt my partner right back? If it's the latter, understand the futility in the impulse. Understand that not only will you possibly end the conversation, but you'll also lose a little moral high ground. ("You said I was being rude to those people at dinner!" *"Yeah? Well, you called* me *an idiot!"*) You don't have to ignore the feeling that you're being attacked, and you don't have to keep it to yourself. In fact, just say it: "I'm feeling attacked right now, and I'm finding it hard to respond to you."

Let's take a typical argument, and run it both ways. First we'll see what happens when the criticized spouse uses the attack response, and then we'll see what happens when the person who feels attacked responds in terms of feelings, *instead* of attacking right back.

The "I Wish You Had Consulted Me" Argument, Nuclear Version

WIFE

Did you have a good time at dinner tonight?

HUSBAND

You know, I *might* have, if you'd have given me any chance to choose our dinner partners. Seems like every time you make dinner plans, you never bother asking *me* where I'd like to go and who I'd like to go out with. And believe me, if I never eat dinner with those people again in this lifetime, that'd suit me *fine*.

(And away we go . . .)

WIFE

Oh, really? Like your friends are such a treat? Gosh, we could've gone *bowling* on a Friday night, or maybe to the bar to watch the game. Please. I thought that couple was a helluva lot more interesting—

HUSBAND

Interesting? The only thing that's interesting is how you would choose to listen to his pompous drivel about work and her stupid stories about their kids. When did you start wanting to hang around such idiots? What's with you, lately?

And so on, and so on, until our scene ends with the sound of a door slamming. Now, let's rewind the tape, and give the wife a new tool: the ability to stop, breathe, reject the attacking responses that seem so tempting, and instead to speak in terms of what she's feeling.

The "I Wish You Had Consulted Me" Argument— Deweaponized Version

WIFE

Did you have a good time at dinner tonight?

HUSBAND

You know, I *might* have, if you'd have given me any chance to choose our dinner partners. Seems like every time you make dinner plans, you never bother asking *me* where I'd like to go and who I'd like to go out with. And believe me, if I never eat dinner with those people again in this lifetime, that'd suit me *fine*.

(She takes a breath. A deep one.)

WIFE

Okay, I'm feeling attacked right now. The things I want to say to you at the moment would more than likely make *you* feel attacked right back, but they won't solve anything. Obviously, I didn't know you would be so upset about going out with that couple.

HUSBAND

Well, it wasn't *that* bad. I just wish that, before you make plans for us, you'd ask me what it is that *I* want to do. It makes me feel lousy when I'm not even consulted.

WIFE

Thank you for telling me that. I didn't realize it was important to you . . . or that you were this upset.

Ta da! Okay, people aren't always quite that reasonable, but the point remains: if you can take an argument that seems to be heading into the stratosphere of personal attack and keep it grounded in the realm of your own feelings, you stand a much better chance of conflict resolution, as opposed to conflict escalation. It's important to realize that your words have a profound effect on how another person will respond to you. When you talk about how you feel—that is, when you use "I" statements instead of "you" statements—you substantially decrease the chance that the person you're talking to will feel attacked. And you substantially increase the chance that they'll want to help you solve the problem at hand.

> It's important to realize that your words have a profound effect on how another person will respond to you.

Another way to think about the *Keep Your Cool* rule is that it's all about the difference between the carrot and the stick. Whatever type of communication you're having with your partner, whether it's an argument or a negotiation, is going to go better when attacks are avoided in favor of incentives. In our little dialogue above, the incentive was a chance to have the conversation be productive, instead of destructive. When our fictitious wife responded to her husband's criticism with a statement about her feelings, she was really offering up an olive branch: "You hurt me, but that doesn't have to mean war."

I know a woman, Alison, who keeps her cool in an altogether different way, but with equally positive results. She's a master of inversion; that is, when Alison hears a criticism, she can often turn it around and make the person doing the criticizing actually feel *good,* drop the complaint, and give her what she wants. Not long ago, her husband Michael fired the first shot in the typical "you paid *what* for that dress?" marital spat, and rather than responding with what was going through her head—"how did you get so *cheap?*"—she said, "It *was* a little more expensive than what I'd normally spend, but I wanted to look great for you." Pretty brilliant, actually: Alison managed to acknowledge the substance of her husband's complaint *and* to make him feel good in a whole other way, as well. (And yes, it's possible to say that she demeaned herself a little when she appealed to Michael in this way. But put the value judgment aside, and understand that this is meant to illustrate the relationship of stimulus to response. She chose the carrot, and not the stick, and made a fight evaporate before it could fully materialize.)

If you find yourself riding London's vast Underground— here in New York, we call it the subway—you'll doubtless hear a recorded announcement while you're standing on the platform warning you to *Mind the Gap*. Who knew that such terrific safety advice works so well when it comes to communication? In the Underground, the phrase refers to the space between the train car and the platform; "mind the gap" means don't trip or get stuck in the hazard zone. For our purposes, it means pretty much the same thing: in communicating with a partner, there is a gap between where you are and where they are, and in that gap there are all kinds of hazards that can cause serious injury. Those hazards come in the form of what we'd call "hot buttons."

When Alison chose to avoid making a crack about what she perceives as her husband's penny-pinching ways, she minded the gap. She understood that Michael has his own unique personality—as we all do—and with that personality comes strengths, weaknesses, and areas of vulnerability. One of his areas of vulnerability is the notion of cheapness; Michael grew up in a household where money was tight, and where his mother constantly called his father a "cheap bastard." Had Alison used the same phrase, or some variation on the theme, Michael would have felt attacked. Because she managed to respond to his criticism in a way that didn't either purposefully or accidentally "push his buttons," he was able to hear what she had to say. Clearly, Alison understands not just communication rules, but also relationship rules: she used the information she had compiled about her husband's personality *(Know the Other)* so as not to be overly offended by his remark. That is, she knows that when he gets upset about money, he's reacting far more to old ghosts than to his current partner. Then she used these last two communication rules we've been discussing *(Keep Your Cool* and *Mind the Gap)* to keep her husband's unkind—though minor—comment from turning into a nasty fight.

Communication, properly understood, has two parts: content (what's being said or conveyed) and process (how it's being said or conveyed). The content is the specific message: "Pass the salt" is what you say when you want someone to . . . well, pass the salt. *How* you say something—even something as mundane as "pass the salt"—can mean the difference between a mutually enhancing experience or an angry, hostile one. (My favorite line in the first *Addams Family* movie comes when young Wednesday Addams makes that exact request: "Pass the salt." Her mother, Morticia, raises her eyebrow and says, "And what do we say?" to which Wednesday chillingly—and hilariously—replies, *"Now."*)

How you say something is the *process* of communication, and is often where that communication goes wrong. Even benign content issues, such as dinner reservations, wallpaper choices, or which TV show to watch can explode into arguments if the process of communicating the content leads to angry, accusing, or provocative feelings. For instance, let's look at an all-too-common complaint that one spouse will have about another: the perpetually empty gas tank. The content of the communication is "I need you to fill the tank when it's low." The process—the argument starter—is often some variation on, "Well, once again I had to stop on the way to work because the car was on fumes. Would it kill you to fill it up, once in awhile? Could you think of somebody else, for a change?" That's really the content (the tank was low and it was an inconvenience) plus strongly worded accusations of laziness and selfishness.

Next time you find yourself in the early stages of an argument with someone—it doesn't matter if it's a romantic partner, a friend, or some guy selling you tires—take a moment to separate out the content from the process. See if you can make a case for *how* you're communicating having a positive impact on *what* you're communicating. Is the process by which you're sharing information more likely to help you walk away from the conversation feeling good . . . or lousy? Keeping an eye on the process, and not allowing yourself to make the other person feel attacked by the way you're imparting information, is critical to keeping your relationship rooted in positive feelings.

You know, while we're looking at the process of communication, let's take a moment to think about the communication of *process:* the art of talking about how things are going. A former mayor of New York was known for this; Ed Koch's catchphrase throughout his tenure at City Hall was, "How'm I doing?" It was a remarkably successful tactic by the mayor, because it gave his constituents the belief that he cared about what they thought, and that their responses could shape the direction of his policies.

> Posing the question "How do you think we're doing?" is something Bernie recommends to all of his married patients.

It works the same way when it's used in the context of a romantic relationship, of course. Posing the question "How do you think we're doing?" is something Bernie recommends to all of his married patients, because it gives each partner a chance to clear the air about the things that trouble them, and it gives each partner a chance to validate the other's grievances. Used with some regularity, the phrase "How are we doing?" creates an ongoing communication about process . . . which ultimately acts as a release valve for the pressures that can build up between partners. Yes, the question invites criticism, but it also makes clear that the person who's asking it is interested in the state of the relationship and wants to enhance it. Not a bad starting point for any conversation, when you think about it.

Talking Pointers

Now that we've spent some time with the four basic rules of communicating, let's take a quick look at some additional tips that can help you navigate just about any important conversation. Since relating with a partner (or a boss, or a parent, or a friend) is about give-and-take, it never hurts to brush up on your negotiating skills.

Be Prepared

Know how you would like the conversation to go, and know what you'd like to avoid. Play it out in your head. The more arguments you can anticipate—and figure out how to answer ahead of time—the more confidence you'll have going in.

Look 'Em in the Eye

While we're on the subject of confidence, here's a way to show some. Eye contact is the quickest way to sell someone on the idea that you're in control. Looking at the floor or letting your eyes wander when you talk to a person gives them the idea that either you're unsure of what you're saying, or that you're not being honest.

Always Avoid "Never," and Never Say "Always"

It is absolutely true: absolutes are almost never true. When you say to someone "Oh, you *always* do this . . ." or "You *never* do that . . ." it's far too easy for them to respond with, "Well, I might *often* (or *rarely*) do the thing you're talking about, but you're wrong to be so absolute. And since you're wrong about *that,* why should I take the rest of what you have to say seriously?"

The Seven-Day Rule

There is one magic phrase that often marks the beginning of the end of a conversation: "Oh, yeah? Well, remember that time that *you* . . ." If you start bringing up things that happened more than a week ago, you sound like you're trying to get even rather than make a point. Keep your conversation focused on the present, because constantly looking backward makes it very hard to move forward.

Have a Talk, Not a Yell

Volume—in the "loudness" sense of the word—is not your friend when you're trying to convince someone of something. In fact, I once knew a man who could dominate business meetings by barely speaking above a whisper. He talked so softly that people had to lean forward in their chairs and listen carefully just to hear him. Make people concentrate on what you're saying, and not on an obnoxious tone of voice.

No Detours, No Shortcuts

Converse the way your English teacher made you answer essay questions: introduce your subject, make your argument, and then cite supporting evidence. You don't get extra points for extra words; a brief and concise argument is a lot more compelling than one in which your main point gets lost in a sea of jibber-jabber.

But by the same token, don't take shortcuts and leave important things out of a conversation in the hope that it will be over quicker. You rarely get "do-overs" when you're having important talks, so make the best, fullest argument you can. (That way, if you don't end up getting what you want, you won't have to make yourself feel even worse by playing the "woulda, coulda, shoulda" game.)

Admit When You're Wrong

When you acknowledge a mistake, you become instantly credible in the eyes of the person you're talking to; you show that you're honest and reasonable. If you *can't* admit when you're wrong, it makes you seem either stubborn or not-too-bright. To win the war, be prepared to gracefully lose a few battles here and there.

When in Doubt, Close Your Mouth

My friend Pete can talk about *anything*. Raise a subject, and he has an opinion. Ask a question, and he has an answer. Like so many people, Pete doesn't let a little thing such as lack of knowledge get in the way of his motormouth, and his ignorance about most things becomes obvious five minutes into any conversation he has. So no one takes him seriously, or listens to what he has to say.

Remember that silence, or a well-timed "I'll have to think about it," won't weaken your argument. But winging it will.

If You're Not Getting Anywhere, Don't Go Any Further

No matter how hard you try, sometimes conversations don't go . . . well, they just don't go. People get frustrated, voices get raised, and bad feelings overtake good intentions. Here's how to avoid that: end the conversation. Acknowledge that you're not getting any-where, tell the person that the subject is important to you, and ask if you can take some time off and come back to it. Respectful disengagement can go a long way toward getting you a fair hearing when the conversation starts up again.

We began the previous chapter with three guidelines meant to help you assess and enhance a relationship: *Know Thyself, Know the Other,* and *Know the Process.* Let's circle back around for a bit, and apply what we've just learned about communication to each of those guidelines.

Communicate Thyself

We all have our secrets, keeping significant parts of our-selves hidden. We do so because we've been burned by reveal-ing ourselves to others, or we're afraid of being ridiculed or berated, or—worst of all—being ignored. Think about all the car rides you've taken where, whether you were with your mom, your friend, or your partner, you let miles go by in to-tal silence, each afraid to share your thoughts. Maybe you were worried about rejection, or you were embarrassed. Maybe you were terrified that your secret thoughts would bore your companion. There are all kinds of reasons for *not* communi-cating your feelings and ideas.

In fact, the closer you are with someone, the more anxiety you're likely to feel about sharing your personal thoughts with them. Especially the troubling stuff, such as feelings of vulnerability, self-doubt, anxiety, or even overconfidence. You don't want to share those things because you want your partner to have the highest possible opinion of you. Which would make sense, if it weren't so entirely wrongheaded: to be close with someone, you need to be comfortable revealing every part of yourself, the troubling things as well as all those great qualities you have. Think of it this way: would you rather have a superficial understanding of your partner, where all of their faults and weaknesses are edited out, or do you want to know who they really are? If you choose the former, you might as well be their friend or coworker, for all the intimacy such a relationship would engender. Nope, I'm betting you're in for the whole package.

Which means you've got to be willing to share *your* whole package. If a relationship is to grow and develop, a couple needs to be willing to discuss not only their hopes and dreams, but also their doubts and concerns. The key is for each partner to hear what the other has to say with respect and empathy, not with defensiveness or criticism. When that happens, then both partners will learn to feel safe enough to reveal themselves. This kind of sharing is key: as we've seen, the more each of you knows about the other, the more you can both predict (and avoid) each other's hot buttons. The more you can do that, the better your communication will be. And yes, the better your communication, the better your relationship. When you choose to communicate your whole self to your partner, you're taking a really important first step in strengthening your romantic bond.

Communicate the Other

Since no one is closer to your partner than you are—both physically and emotionally—no one is in a better position to observe your partner. You do it constantly, whether you realize it or not. Over time, you make some excellent observations about their behavior, and some accurate predictions about how they'll act in a given situation. That's all helpful knowledge, so why not share the wealth? Granted, there are observations you'll make that might not do them any good, and you ought to weigh the other's feelings before approaching them with any of your insights. Most of what you observe, though, can prove relationship-enhancing when it's presented in the proper way.

For the record, the proper way means that you first ask your partner if they're interested in hearing your observation about them, and then—if they've answered in the affirmative—that you're careful to use the phrase "It seems to me . . ." as a preface to whatever it is you have to say. Remember: you're not criticizing, you're offering up information with the intention of helping them and your relationship. How you present that information will make all the difference in their willingness to hear it.

You can *Communicate the Other*—let your partner or spouse know what you observe about them—at any point in your relationship. In fact, one of Bernie's patients recently told him she'd had great success with this particular guideline in dealing with her husband of thirty-five years. Here's how it worked, for her:

Throughout the course of their marriage, Leslie and Paul Park had followed the same pattern: Paul would become quiet, reclusive, or noncommunicative, and Leslie would become angry with him for it. She'd yell at him in exasperation, and he, in turn, would get in the car and take off, not telling her where he was heading . . . leaving Leslie feeling nervous and rejected. Each time, he would return within several hours, and they would avoid speaking about the confrontation. Within a few months, they'd repeat the process.

Until one day when Leslie skipped the anger part, and made an observation to her husband: "It seems to me that we go through the same thing pretty often. When I get angry with you, you withdraw. I'd like to know why you withdraw. It would really help me." Her husband got silent—which she expected—but he stayed in the room with her, which she didn't expect. After a while, he answered her. It turns out that when he was very young, Paul learned that the only way to stop his mother's frequent anger toward him would be to go to his room and be very quiet. He would remove himself to end his mother's tirades. Leslie thanked him for telling her, and then told him that when he removed himself from her, it made her anxious.

And he got it. He understood. As they talked some more, they came upon a way of avoiding their chronic fight: Paul offered to let her know when he felt one of his quiet spells coming on, and she told him she'd respect them and not badger him about them. (Hence, he wouldn't get in his car and disappear, making her feel rejected.) Over time, Paul found himself able to go to his wife about some of the things causing his periods of withdrawal, because he was no longer afraid that his quiet spells would make her angry.

Actually, Leslie managed to apply communication skills to two of the three rules for assessing and improving relationships: *Know the Other* and *Know the Process.* (And, in fact, you could make a case for the fact that she used all three, because in telling Paul what happened to her, emotionally, during his absences, she used *Know Thyself,* as well.) Leslie made an observation about Paul's behavior, but she also managed to *Communicate the Process.* She talked to her husband about the repeated interactions that characterized their marriage . . . rather than getting bogged down in discussing the details of any one of his many periods of withdrawal. Essentially, she turned a *you* conversation ("What's wrong with *you?*") into an *us* conversation ("How can *we* fix this thing that keeps happening between *us?*"). While communicating the process didn't resolve the Parks' chronic issue overnight, it did open a new and very healthy dialogue between them that eventually caused the silence-to-anger-to-screeching-tires-to-anxiety routine to end. He still gets quiet, from time to time, but she no longer takes it personally.

Sometimes, communicating the process can resolve chronic problems in an instant. My friend Mary Sue has an investment banker for a husband, and not long after their marriage she noticed they'd developed a chronic dinnertime pattern: he'd come home sullen after a particularly hard day at the office, and find some reason to start a fight. Either she'd say or do something he didn't like, or—if he couldn't find an immediate reason to bark at her—he'd bring up some recent problem, and start fighting about it all over again. She would defend or explain herself, but his mood wouldn't improve. Finally, she realized that their fights were never about what they seemed to be about; they were about his lousy mood. So one night she told him: "I know you had a bad day at work, and I'd really like to hear about it, if you want to tell me. But don't take it out on me, okay?" And he did the damndest thing: he stopped, mid-complaint, and apologized. It's now a joke between them. When he comes home noticeably unhappy, she says something like, "I'm guessing that now would *not* be a good time to tell you that I lost all our money playing Internet poker?" He laughs ruefully, and then tells her about his day.

We teach our kids early on that fighting, kicking, scratching, and the like are not good ways to deal with anger or to problem-solve; instead, we tell them, "use your words." We tell them to communicate, because talking things through is the way to relieve the anger and anxiety that started the problem in the first place. What's amazing is how often we—the adults—don't manage to internalize the lesson: we may not be kicking and scratching, but we forget that early, extremely useful piece of advice. We forget to use our words.

So far, we've looked at the rules and guidelines for assessing and improving our relationship through observation and communication. Before we move on, though, let's look at what happens when we ignore these rules and guidelines, and use one of the three classically bad methods of handling the conflict that can arise in a romantic relationship: *Not Communicating, Communicating with Outsiders,* and *Having an Affair.*

Forgive the stilted grammar of the phrase *Not Communicating,* but I've used it on purpose. Not communicating is not the same as silence; it refers to the selective "leaving out" of information. In other words, a couple may be communicating plenty in terms of their bad feelings and disappointments—there may be a flood of words between them—but somehow they manage to filter out anything positive or constructive, anything that would make the other partner feel appreciated, loved, or secure. Likewise, there are partners that talk incessantly about their mutual good feelings, but avoid discussing anything that doesn't fit in with their fantasy-fueled "perfect" relationship. Which, of course, means that the little problems they're avoiding eventually turn into great big honkin' problems that explode as if from out of nowhere.

When you keep your feelings—positive *or* negative—to yourself, you end up isolating your partner. Face it: they *know* when you're keeping things from them, and in the absence of the actual information, they might tend to imagine the worst. Your secrets distance them by making

> When you keep your feelings—positive *or* negative—to yourself, you end up isolating your partner.

them feel untrustworthy—or worse, unloved. A partner's growing paranoia is a common result of *Not Communicating*.

There are two other common results from keeping things inside you: somatic distress (which is a fancy way of saying physical symptoms) and "acting out." Somatic distress is something we've all experienced, from a headache or backache brought on by stress to the stomach cramps that plague us when we're anxious. There are as many possible psychosomatic symptoms as there are problems that cause them. Acting out, though, is a little harder to spot. Bernie points to the classic example of the patient who chose to end an argument with his wife by simply telling her he was no longer angry, even though he was. They were on their way to a restaurant, and he didn't want to spoil the evening. Big mistake: not a half hour later, he acted out by sneaking a hot pepper into her soup when she wasn't looking. She gagged, sputtered, realized what her husband had done, and was furious. "What an angry thing to do!" she yelled. Embarrassed, he mumbled something about how she couldn't take a joke. His unconscious acting out—playing a hostile "prank" on his wife—ended up doing the thing he thought he was avoiding by consciously suppressing his anger in the car: it ruined the evening.

Here's the beauty of having a friend, a bartender, or a manicurist to share your troubles with: you get to tell your side of the story without fear of recrimination or contradiction. You get to present your litany of complaints, injustices, and hurts, uninterrupted, to someone who more than likely will nod and tell you how put upon you are. Pretty good gig, huh?

Well, not really. When you *Communicate to Outsiders* the things that are troubling you about your relationship, you're unwittingly damaging that relationship in a few different ways. First, you're reinforcing your own self-righteousness while downplaying your role in the creation of any problems you have with your partner, which makes you even more resistant to listen and compromise when you're actually communicating with your partner. Ah, if I had a nickel for every time a spouse has heard some variation of "Well, you know what? Everyone I've told this story to agrees with *me*." Spouses hear it, therapists hear it, and all it really proves is that the speaker is talking to the wrong people about his or her relationship woes.

Second, when you choose to discuss your problems with an outsider, you're reducing your motivation to discuss those issues with your partner. You're getting some minor amount of relief—it feels good to get stuff off your chest—but that relief is coming from the wrong source, and having the wrong effect. When you get that temporary surge of good feelings, you lull yourself into a false sense that the relationship is better. It's as if you just needed to unburden yourself . . . and you no longer need to discuss the issue with your partner. As if. Get ready to be knocked on your rear end when that temporarily abated difficulty inevitably comes roaring back, stronger than ever.

The easiest way to nuke your own relationship, of course, is by *Having an Affair*. Cheating on a partner or a spouse is destructive in any number of ways, from creating feelings of betrayal to eroding trust, but let's put aside the ethical stuff and examine specifically how an affair perpetuates conflict and patterns of negative relating between partners.

From a psychological standpoint, an extramarital (or extramonogamous) affair perpetuates the illusion that the cause of any marital conflict is the other person . . . the spouse that's being cheated on. To understand how that happens, let's remember the nature of a committed relationship: it's the bond that's created when two people who've gone through the idealization and reality phases decide to accept both the positive and negative aspects of each other's personality in order to move the relationship forward. When you commit to someone, you commit to their liabilities as well as their assets, their weaknesses as well as their strengths. Because this is the case, conflict resolution between you means you have to deal with the "bad" in your partner, as well as the "good," just as they have to with you.

> Conflict resolution between you means you have to deal with the "bad" in your partner, as well as the "good," just as they have to with you.

Which is a dynamic that changes the instant you decide to have an affair. (Once again, I'm not picking on you. It's just easier to type "you" instead of "you or your partner." The point remains the same no matter who's doing the cheating.) When you become involved with another person, you effectively split the idea of "good" and "bad" into two different people: your new lover becomes the "good" while that spouse you're so clearly unhappy with morphs into the "bad." Think about it: people who have affairs *always* talk about their lovers in the most positive and endearing terms, swearing up and down that all their needs are (finally!) being met by this new person. The spouse they're cheating on is spoken of as if they're the source of all dissatisfaction, the source of all problems. Which, of course, is a screwy form of idealization, wherein the lover takes on the attributes of the projected "perfect" person, while the spouse is now the recipient of the cheater's every negative projection.

An ongoing love affair perpetuates and reinforces this split between "good" and "bad." The cuckolded spouse can't stick up for him or herself, because anything they do or say is seen by the cheating spouse through the warped perspective of projected fantasy: "I don't have to listen to you; it's your fault I'm cheating on you in the first place." At the same time, the person having the affair can't lose, in a sense, because they now have someone (their lover) who will reaffirm their self-righteousness by agreeing with all the bad stuff the cheater is saying about their spouse.

The sad reality of an affair is that it's really just an unconscious attempt on the part of the cheating spouse to get back to the idealized positive transference stage of a relationship. It's an attempt to skip out on the hard reality of an existing long-term commitment by jumping right into the idealization phase of a relationship with someone else. It effectively kills any chance of righting the wrongs in the marital or committed relationship, because that relationship can never live up to the fantasized perfection of the affair.

Unfortunately, the end of an affair doesn't necessarily make things better between spouses. Even if the affair has never been discovered, the spouse who indulged in it holds on

to some part of the good/bad fantasy: in other words, just because their lover is now gone doesn't mean that they're suddenly willing to concede that their long-term partner brings
good, positive things to their relationship. When the affair
has been discovered, of course, the spouse who's been cheated
on will recall the hurt for the duration of the marriage. Arguments years later can still result in the rearousal of the hurt
and anguish caused by the affair. It's just incredibly hard to
find a good outcome, once an affair has happened to a marriage.

Unless, of course, you're the spouse that's been cheated
on, and your partner actually leaves you to marry their lover.
Because you know what'll happen? Your (now) ex will finally
get a chance to go beyond the idealization phase with their
paramour . . . and then wind up miserable all over again,
when they discover how wrong they were to decide their issues with you were all your fault. (Okay, that's not a "good"
outcome; it's just one that will make *you* feel really good, if
you've been cheated on.)

Any one of these three methods, *Not Communicating, Communicating with Outsiders,* or *Having an Affair,* can effectively
end a committed relationship. The problem is, ending that
relationship won't solve the riddle of what made it go bad in
the first place. Breaking up doesn't help reveal what it is in
the unconscious of each of the partners that caused the relationship's underlying issues. While a breakup can have an immediate effect of relief—"Lord, I'm finally free of *that*
nonsense"—it's never a lasting effect: left unexamined and

not fully dealt with, the nonsense will most likely reappear in any new relationship.

So let's back away from breaking up as an option. Let's assume that you're reading this book in the hopes of understanding how to cope with a relationship that has its fair share of problems, but also retains some level of good feeling. (Which, you'll be relieved to know, is the definition of a salvageable relationship.) Relationship repair and enhancement will require some serious effort, of course, and it will require adherence to the rules of communication that we've just discussed. It will require each of you to accept the personality flaws of the other . . . and to tread lightly around the other's "hot spots."

Quite possibly, it will also involve professional intervention. Which, when I write it that way, seems scary: "professional intervention" sounds as if it should come with anesthesia. So let me withdraw the phrase and start the paragraph over.

Quite possibly, repairing your relationship will involve finding someone who can help you and your partner understand the unconscious causes of your troubles, learn to communicate more constructively, and feel better about your relationship. In other words, you might need someone trained as a coach, a referee, and a cheerleader. That's a good general description of a couples therapist, though I suspect Bernie bristles at the idea that his job description includes the word *cheerleader.* But he'll have to get over it: offering encouragement from the sidelines is a noble part of what he does. In our next chapter, we'll take a look at the rest of what he does in his role as a couples therapist.

The Best Relationship Advice You'll Ever Get (From a Movie You've Never Heard Of)

Solid wisdom comes from the weirdest sources. Case in point: there I was, sitting in one of those great old Manhattan movie theaters in 1978, trying to figure out whether or not Shelly Brooks wanted me to hold her hand, when one of the best pieces of life-and-love advice I would ever hear came spilling from the mouth of a secondary character in a third-rate World War II movie.

I'll get to the advice in a moment. First, let me set it up by giving you a synopsis of *Force 10 from Navarone*, one of the lower points in Harrison Ford's career. In the film, Ford and a few other guys try to slow the Nazi march across Europe by destroying a key Yugoslavian bridge. This being a Hollywood production, they don't simply try to blow up the bridge, they decide to blow up a dam upstream from the bridge, so that the producers can justify some very, very bad special effects. (Raging waters destroy bridge, Nazi tanks fall into river, and so on.)

At the climax of the movie, Ford and Robert Shaw—the guy who played Quint in *Jaws*—sneak into the bowels of the dam to plant explosives. Realizing they've run out of time and the Nazis are almost to that downstream bridge, they set the timer on the charge for twenty seconds. In other words, they heroically turn their job into a suicide mission. Only the explosion doesn't blow a hole in the dam. They're knocked out, and when they come to, they hightail it out of that dam, cursing Edward Fox, their explosives expert, who sits on the hillside above, remarkably sanguine about the lack of visible damage below. The fourth member of their team sits next to him, furious at the failure. "We've been through all this and . . . nothing!" he screams. (Shelly pointed out that considering the surrounding woods were crawling with Nazis, screaming probably wasn't a great idea.) Fox smiles, lights his pipe, and says, "You've got to let nature take her course. It'll work; give it time."

Which is the advice I promised you. *It'll work; give it time.*

In the movie, it plays out like this: a little crack appears in the bowels of the dam, and some water trickles through. The water pressure makes the crack grow, more water comes, and so on, until chunks of concrete are flying every which way. Eventually the whole thing collapses, the Nazis get wet, and Harrison Ford goes on to the greener pastures of Indiana Jones and the *Star Wars* movies.

Years later, I thought of that silly movie and Edward Fox's words, several days after a particularly uncomfortable business meeting. With my dad. (Have I mentioned that I was once masochistic enough to work in a family business?) I'd done everything I could to make what I thought was a very good marketing point, only to be rebuffed in front of a conference room full of executives. I walked out of that meeting angry as hell, feeling like a failure. Mostly because my dad-boss didn't even acknowledge that what I had to say made good strategic sense.

And then a few days later, water started trickling through a crack. Pop asked me into his office, and let me make a second argument, which he again rejected. But a little more slowly this time. A few days after that, he gave in completely. The dam collapsed. Fox's words came back to me: "You've got to let nature take her course. It'll work; give it time." I'd been so intent on getting my way on the spot that I'd forgotten a very basic truth about communication, which is that you have to allow your words a chance to sink in, sometimes. You have to let people *internalize* what you're saying; once they've made your thoughts and words their own, they're far more likely to *listen* to them.

Eventually, it dawned on me that the *give it time* strategy might work with my wife, too. Though I didn't magically start winning every argument—patience, after all, isn't a substitute for being right—I did start to feel a lot less stress when we argued. Here's why: I stopped worrying about having the last word, and instead concentrated on being as clear as I could (and as calm as I could) about my thoughts and feelings. I no longer worried that every argument had to be settled on the spot, and so I lost that sense of desperation that can cause some people (read: yours truly) to say stupid or unkind things in frustration. Things that certainly don't help win arguments.

Funny thing about applying patience to communication: once you stop worrying about blowing up your partner's arguments and instead allow some time for your words to do their work, you find yourself much more willing and able to let your partner's words do their work on *you*. And suddenly, you're having discussions, and not fights.

8.

Your CPU in the ICU:
Couples Therapy,
Demystified

L et's say you have a friend who starts behaving very strangely. Maybe she makes a scene in public over something supremely trivial; perhaps she shuts herself behind closed doors for a couple of days, jeopardizing her job, her friendships, and her romantic relationship. You see that behavior, and you slap a perfectly understandable label on it: you declare that your friend is acting *psycho*.

And according to therapists who believe in the power of the unconscious, you're not that far off in your terminology. Your friend's behavior, a doctor such as Bernie would tell you, is more accurately *psychodynamic* in nature.

Don't be put off by the ten-dollar word: psychodynamics simply refers to the school of psychological thought we've been looking at over the course of this book, the one that tells us that personality is a mix of conscious and unconscious forces, created through the internalization of early experiences. (In plain English: the psychodynamic approach holds that the things that happen to you early in life get filed away—both the good stuff that you remember and the bad stuff that maybe you don't—and they wind up motivating your behavior later in life. So the more you can recall and understand those experiences, the more you can understand why you do the things you do, choose the partners that you choose, have the fights that you have, and so on.)

The term *psychodynamics* refers to a school of thought, but it also refers to a process that's constantly going on in your mind: an interaction among the unconscious components of your personality. Think of the thoughts, feelings, fantasies, and behaviors created by your early childhood experiences as separate forces, each vying for control of you. That's psychodynamics in action. If you need a visual, picture the old movie cliché—probably most famously used in *Animal House*—of a guy with a tiny angel sitting on one shoulder and a tiny devil sitting on the other, each urging him on in an opposing direction. Obviously, most of us aren't quite so torn, and our impulses aren't usually so completely opposite as to be easily represented by an angel and a devil. Still, you get the point: the psychodynamic approach holds that your impulses and actions are dictated by forces within your personality, forces that are largely unconscious and very deeply rooted.

Whether those forces are positive or negative, they're formed by building blocks known as psychodynamic units. Each unit is made up of a complete childhood memory—that is, not just the recollection but also the emotion that comes with it. Think of a happy experience from when you were young. Maybe it's your eighth birthday party, or a trip you took with your family to an amusement park. Notice how the memory can make you relive the good feeling that the experience brought to you the first time? Now think of something uncomfortable or painful from growing up—for me, that covers the better part of junior high—and you'll notice that the act of remembering brings with it some part of the painful feeling state along with the details of what happened. It's that combination of specific content and feeling state that makes up a psychodynamic unit.

Most of the psychodynamic units that we carry around are formed in relation to . . . well, our relations. Since we spend most of our early life interacting with family, those interactions take on the greatest weight in our developing personality. If our interactions are generally positive, and we carry around more good units than bad ones, then chances are good that we'll eventually select a romantic partner with whom we can have a satisfying, positive relationship. If our early relationships were painful and difficult, however, then we run a far greater chance of having our negative psychodynamic units interfere with future romantic happiness.

We've looked at some of the ways that our unconscious bubbles up into our awareness from time to time, by way of dreams, Freudian slips, repetitive behavior patterns, and so on. But those are the exceptions: most of the time, we are blissfully unaware of the pressures those psychodynamic units that exist in our unconscious are putting on us. We do things every day that have no clear, rational motivation, but we don't question (or even notice) most of those things, either because they aren't so upsetting that we feel the need to look for what caused them, or because there already seems to be a perfectly logical explanation handy.

Which explains why we're so clueless about romantic attraction. When we first choose someone as a love object, whether it's across a crowded bar, or at work, or on a blind date, we do it (we believe) because that person is good-looking, well-dressed, sexy, funny, kind, or any combination of a whole lot of concrete, rational reasons. Psychodynamics tells us, though, that our stated reasons are a smoke screen: we really choose someone based on a very complicated and unconscious process through which we recognize ways that our personalities might mesh. Again, this can be a good thing ("You will complete me") or it can be a bad thing ("You'll treat me as badly as my lousy self-image tells me I deserve to be treated"). It all comes down to the ratio between our good psychodynamic units and our bad ones.

As a couple starts dating and then moves through the various phases of a relationship, each inevitably activates unconscious, psychodynamic forces in the other. Not at first, of course. At first, each partner idealizes the other, which activates only the positive stuff: this is how a strong romantic bond is formed. By the time the couple reaches the reality stage, though, the negative stuff starts surfacing and in time can include feelings of anger, anxiety, depression, and so on. Eventually, the positive and negative units that each has unearthed in the other exist side by side, kind of like a checklist of pros and cons. If each of the partners experiences more positive psychodynamic units than negative ones as a result of the relationship, then that relationship feels gratifying and loving. If each feels mostly bad stuff, then the relationship is conflicted and unsatisfying.

And if either comes in contact with the other's flashpoint, then look out. Think of a flashpoint as that one particular hot spot, that one frayed psychological nerve that each of us has. It's whatever issue caused us the most discomfort as a child, and was therefore sent packing into the deepest, darkest part of our unconscious . . . where it became the one psychodynamic unit that can most easily and reliably ignite our anger and anxiety. Remember my friend on the basketball court, the guy who's dad told him he was the stupidest kid in town? I'd bet the farm that his flashpoint is reached—causing him to experience horrible feelings of worthlessness—whenever his romantic partner talks down to him, or in any way makes him feel dumb. He doesn't know that those feelings are programmed into him thanks to his dad, he just knows he feels really awful (and then really angry) when someone finds his flashpoint, and so he reacts out of proportion to the actual slight.

Are you starting to get the picture about why fights with romantic partners seem so much worse than any other kind of conflict? In a long-term relationship, it's inevitable that the partners will (unwittingly) discover and trigger each other's flashpoints, causing arguments that are far more hostile than their stated causes would suggest they should be. That's an important distinction: it's often not what a couple is arguing about that splits them up or sends them into counseling, it's *how* they're arguing. In relationships that are characterized by generally good feelings, each person's flashpoint is rarely triggered, and arguments tend to be infrequent and manageable. In more conflicted relationships, fighting starts to follow a pattern in which both partners' flashpoints get triggered . . . causing all kinds of additional stress.

> It's often not what a couple is arguing about that splits them up or sends them into counseling, it's *how* they're arguing.

That pattern is something Bernie calls the "central psychodynamic unit," or CPU, of a relationship. It's odd, I know, to use psychodynamic unit in relation to individuals *and* to couples, but it makes sense: when your psychodynamic units rub up against those of your partner, they create all new units that are unique to the two of you as a couple. When your most negative psychodynamic units—your respective flashpoints—rub up against each other, they create a CPU. Think of a CPU as the blueprint for all of the fights that you have with your partner, a blueprint that's followed no matter what any given argument is seemingly about.

To give you an idea of what I mean by that, here are some examples of the CPUs that couples bring into Bernie's office just about every week:

"It doesn't matter what we're discussing. I'm always wrong, and he's always right."

"No matter what we're fighting about, she immediately explodes and I immediately withdraw."

"The minute we start arguing, he attacks me. So I have no choice but to attack him right back."

"If I disagree with anything she says, she gets very insecure, and wants to drop the subject. I end up spending my time reassuring her that I still love her and that everything will work out, and we never actually talk about whatever it was we were disagreeing over."

I could list examples for the next 682 pages (and beyond), because relationship CPUs come in infinite varieties. What each example has in common is that the particular issue being argued over—money, having children, taking out the trash, and so on—is irrelevant; it's the characteristic pattern of interaction (the CPU) that leads to chronic relationship trouble.

Some couples—those in Rel-Con One and sometimes Rel-Con Two marriages—manage to intuitively avoid pushing each other's buttons; over time, they learn techniques that help them resolve conflict with relative ease, so they can go right back to their warm, loving, and affectionate relationships. Couples that find themselves arguing chronically, though, have a much harder time navigating their way back to the good stuff. This is when Bernie's phone tends to ring.

Partners seek out couples therapy when their pattern of relating causes such pain that each one sees the other as producing far more negative feelings than positive ones. The therapist's couch is often described by people as "a last resort," before they seriously consider ending the relationship. (That sounds dire, but if you look at it the right way, it's also hopeful: for a couple to choose an attempt at counseling over jumping right into divorce court, there have to be memories of more positive relating, and a belief that there's some chance at returning the relationship to its former, happy status.) What a couple looks for in a therapist is someone who can intervene in their chronically negative interaction and get them back on the road to positive and effective relating.

Which is a pretty tall order. Just about every couple that seeks a marriage or relationship counselor shares one common trait: each partner has a near-total inability to be objective or understanding. Each wants to play the role of victim, and blame the other for all of the marital woes. So the therapist has to step into the middle—often tiptoeing, at first—of the couple's flawed process of relating, and try to help them regain some equilibrium.

Here's how couples therapy generally works:

Over the first few sessions, the therapist gets to observe the couple in action. Each partner tends to present themselves in therapy in pretty much the same way they present themselves to each other: it isn't long until they're communicating/arguing/discussing/fighting in front of their therapist in exactly the same way they do when they're alone together. If the therapist is psychodynamic in approach, he or she understands that there are two separate personalities in the relationship, and the unconscious forces in each of those personalities are clashing in a way that produces dysfunction in the relationship. I have put it that way for a purpose: the therapist isn't necessarily looking for answers to the ostensible arguments that the couple is having, he or she is looking to understand the couple's central psychodynamic unit and how that unit is causing the problem that brought them in for therapy.

The way a therapist does this is through observing three

basic things: how the couple relates to each other; how they relate (as individuals and as a unit) to the therapist; and how the therapy is affecting the couple as the sessions go on—are these two people getting along any better? Eventually, the history of the relationship and the family background of each partner starts to emerge in the sessions, both in terms of what the partners reveal and also in what the therapist starts to recognize as the past operating within the relationship. All of this information eventually helps the therapist to diagnose . . .

. . . wait for it . . .

. . . *the relationship.* And that's the rub: couples therapy isn't about "shrinking" people or determining what's wrong with them. It's about understanding breakdowns in methods of communication; it's about finding a path back to better ways of relating. As I wrote in the introduction, Bernie tells patients who approach therapy with some trepidation because of a perceived social stigma about seeking professional help that in couples therapy, *you're* not the patient, your relationship is.

The trick, of course, is to bring your relationship in for a checkup *before* it's on life-support.

> It's about understanding breakdowns in methods of communication; it's about finding a path back to better ways of relating.

Actually, let's trade the medical metaphor for an automotive one, and remember that (as I also wrote in the introduction) relationships are not unlike cars in one basic respect: do a little maintenance at the first sign of trouble, and you might well avoid all kinds of hellish repair down the road. Oddly enough, people often steer clear of mechanics and therapists for the same reason; namely, fear of what they'll find. You know how frightened you can be of that little knocking noise from under the hood, the one that sounds like it's going to cost a fortune to fix? Quite often, it turns out to be a loose fan belt, which is no big deal to take care of. Likewise, many couples who are sure that their relationships are beyond repair are pleasantly surprised to find (through therapy) that even their CPU— their unique way of relating to each other under stress—isn't an entirely negative thing. In fact, in many cases, that CPU can work *for* them, once they understand the dynamic of their relationship and how to work around trouble spots. Here's an example of that, from Bernie's practice:

Jeremy and Margot came to Bernie several years into their marriage, each complaining that the other had "changed" and was no longer trying to keep the relationship strong. In fact, that was about as pleasant as their descriptions got for the first several weeks of therapy. Jeremy, Margot told Bernie, was always angry and attacking, critical of even the smallest things Margot did. For his part, Jeremy accused Margot of making him feel "dead inside" and of being angry as well, and bitingly sarcastic to boot. From Bernie's description of their mutual hostility in early sessions, I suspect that if Jeremy and Margot had been friends of mine, I'd have given them about a 2 percent chance of making it to their next anniversary.

Over time, it came out that Jeremy had grown up in a family in which emotions were not expressed and particularly not tolerated in young Jeremy. The words that he had initially

used to describe his marriage—*dead, empty,* and *depressed*—
started to come out in his descriptions of his internal childhood experiences. Margot's family had also been cold, but in
a full-out rejecting, noncaring way. But rather than become
depressed, Margot had grown up to be a highly emotional
woman, capable of extreme warmth and affection as well as
anger and nasty, biting sarcasm. Earlier in their relationship,
their personalities—defying what you or I might call common sense—meshed in a very positive way: Jeremy counted
on Margot's emotionalism to make him feel alive, and his good
feeling would produce warm, nurturing behavior in him,
which Margot needed. The relationship cruised along, each filling the other's need.

Until Jeremy or Margot would inadvertently screw it all
up. Over the years, several situations arose that made one or
the other incapable of meeting their partner's psychological
needs, which triggered a breakdown in the relationship. For
instance, Margot hit a period of stress in her job, which brought
out feelings of anxiety and depression. She no longer came
home in the happy, upbeat mood that brought out Jeremy's
nurturing. Without that nurturing, her mood would darken
further, often lapsing into the silence that Jeremy had experienced throughout his youth. He would become angry and
critical, causing Margot to reexperience those awful feelings
of rejection she had as a girl.

Essentially, the positive feedback loop that they'd experienced early in their relationship morphed into a negative feedback loop. Which meant that their CPU—their usual method
of relating under stress—was actually a good thing for them,
most of the time. When one or the other would inadvertently

violate the other's psychological need, though, the relationship would start spiraling downward into dysfunction.

In his role as a couples therapist to Jeremy and Margot, Bernie first collected data on their relationship, then evaluated that data (or, if you like, figured out their CPU) so that he could point out to each of them how the things they said and how they said them affected the other. Bernie showed them the nature of their CPU so that they could understand the hurtful and painful feelings they were unwittingly causing each other. Over time, Jeremy and Margot internalized his observations so that they could put what they'd learned to constructive use outside of his office. Ultimately, what Bernie helped the couple to do was to relate to each other and talk in a way that showed more understanding of, and compassion for, their respective problem areas. While they still had fights—counseling isn't a magic bullet, after all—those fights became less intense and shorter in duration.

Though some couples come into therapy insisting that there is a specific issue they can't resolve, it always eventually comes down to a CPU. That CPU may take a number of sessions to fully emerge, but once it does, it emerges in session after session after session. And while it's important to discuss the content of a particular problem, and how to compromise and effectively problem-solve, it's critically important to tackle that CPU, to deal with the unconscious personality forces that are at work in the relationship. As therapy sessions go on, the therapist must constantly ask for feedback— "How's it going?"—to gauge how the relationship is faring outside of the sessions. Though it's a given that there will be lapses and regressions and a continuation of the dysfunctional patterns of relating, you can tell when couples therapy is helping by an increase in the frequency of positive relating. That is, it's working when the fighting is dialed down and the good stuff starts to reemerge.

The ultimate outcome of couples therapy depends on three things: the nature and severity of the personality issues involved, the intensity of the CPU dysfunction, and the ability of the therapist to correctly diagnose the relationship and make the right recommendations. Which means there's no guessing—right up front, at least—how long couples therapy will take, because it depends on so many variables. Like how severe the pain can be from the reactivation of each partner's internalized experiences. And how willing each partner is to look at and recognize the true source of that pain. When you come down to it, the success of couples therapy depends upon the degree to which partners can learn to fulfill each others' psychological needs without experiencing added psychological pain in themselves.

I asked Bernie to tell me about a particularly difficult relationship he'd encountered as a therapist, and he immediately came up with the case of Larry and Stacy Greenhut, whose CPU reared its ugly head in their very first session, and showed up for every one thereafter. Diagnosing their ills wasn't so much of a problem, Bernie told me: it was getting them to break out of their destructive pattern of relating that took a long time.

From the get-go, Stacy was an extremely anxious, nervous person, who tended to panic at even the slightest hint that her husband was disapproving of her. Didn't matter if the subject was her ability to do her job or her ability to pick the right eye shadow; any sign that Larry disagreed with her sent her into what us nonpsychologists would call a tizzy. She seemed to believe that any disapproval (or even negativity) on her husband's part could signal the end of their relationship. So his every opinion carried way too much weight with her, and her anxiety over what his opinion of something would be would cause her to nag him and hurry up and render that opinion already.

Which might not have been so bad, if Larry weren't an almost painfully deliberate man. In fact, Larry was so overcontrolled that Bernie told me he'd lapse into lengthy silences after just about any question; asking Larry his opinion of a movie or a ball game or *the weather* would elicit a carefully considered, slowly given answer. So basically, the Greenhuts' CPU was that Larry would withdraw into thought and Stacy would get more and more anxious. Her anxiety would cause her to badger him, and that would interrupt his thought process . . . dragging it out even longer.

As I said, that CPU came out in sessions in much the same way the old joke says they vote in Chicago: early and often. Even on Bernie's couch, the Greenhuts battled. Bernie would ask Larry a question about his marriage, and Stacy would work herself up into an anxious state, waiting for the answer. Larry would declare that her anxiety was making it too hard for him to think, so he wouldn't be able to answer. There was no way for Bernie to calm either of them down enough to make any progress.

So he separated them. Bernie embarked on separate sessions with each of the Greenhuts, and only then was he able to start the real work of strengthening the relationship. Alone with Bernie—who would not get anxious—Larry was able to become a bit more spontaneous in his responses to questions, and to see how his method of answering things so deliberately created anxiety in his wife. Alone with Bernie, Stacy was able to lower her anxiety and to recognize the childhood causes of that anxiety. She was also able to learn a little patience, and how to compliment her husband on what was, when she thought about it, his thoughtfulness. It was only after these chronic, defensive interpersonal patterns were dealt with that the Greenhuts could resume couples therapy, and learn to provide for each other psychologically in a way that was more gratifying for the relationship.

Most people's CPUs are not as problematic as the Greenhuts'. It's much more common in couples therapy for partners to respond with empathy and compassion once it's pointed out to them how each has been doing or saying things that produce psychological pain in the other . . . pain that has its roots in the internalized past. In other words, folks in couples therapy are often relieved to learn that they really aren't the cause of their partner's pain, and they are able to use that relief in a positive way.

Which is a pretty good way to sum up this book: maybe the title should have been *It Really Isn't Your Fault*. That's not to say that you never do anything wrong in your relationship, or that your partner isn't responsible for the way in which he or she talks to you. Those things are true. But so is this: you each

bring a complex personality into your relationship, a personality made up of stuff that you had little or no control over.
Your unique personality affects you—and ultimately your
relationship—in ways that you can't always see, predict, or
control, at least without some attempt at self-reflection, observation, and understanding. Maybe you'll need a little outside help with your relationship, and there's nothing wrong
with that.

But probably you won't. I used the phrase "couples therapy, demystified" in the title of this chapter, but the truth is,
we've been demystifying what therapists such as Bernie do
throughout this book. In reading this far, you've gotten a basic
understanding of how your personality was formed and how
you choose romantic partners. You've learned how that personality of yours dictates not only your romantic choices, but
also the path of each of your romantic relationships. You've
come to understand why relationships in conflict tend to stay
in conflict. You've also realized that, with some effort, you can
use what you've learned on these pages to help strengthen your
relationship, in pretty much the same way a couples therapist
would.

The point to keep in mind is that you open a book like
this because *you want to make that effort.* Though your relationship woes may seem daunting or even overwhelming, you
have enough memory of the good feelings and satisfaction
that your relationship has brought you in the past that you
want to find ways to minimize the conflict. You want to help
your partner deal with the more troubling stuff in their unconscious, and you want to feel so close to them that you can
open yourself up and let them help you deal with the things

that bother *you*. In the end, you want to repair your relationship so that you and your partner can continue to grow together.

And hopefully put up a united front when your kids start blaming you for all of *their* screwed-up relationships.

The Book of Love,
Reader's Digest Edition

Falling in love may be easy—at least, I remember Linda Ronstadt singing something along those lines—but relationships are complicated. For starters, romantic choice isn't some random event based on physical attraction (or any other surface reason), but rather the result of a complex process by which you unconsciously recognize personality traits in the other that will somehow mesh with your own. From the very instant of attraction, you start off on a course that has both predictable patterns—if you know what to look for—and clearly defined phases.

The ways in which you'll relate to your partner are derived from your earlier relationships. That is, your *way* earlier relationships—those that existed with your mom and dad, brothers and sisters, and anyone else you had regular contact with as a young child. These are the folks that weighed the heaviest in the formation of your personality . . . and it's that very personality that determines not only who you choose, romantically, but also how smooth (or not) the course of your love will be. Your personality was created in four basic steps:

1. You were born into a specific set of interpersonal relationships. (You and your mom, you and your dad, you and your sister, and so on.)
2. The members of your family related to you in ways determined partially by your temperament, but even more so by their own personalities, which were formed largely by how *they* were parented.
3. The consistent aspects of your early relationships, both good and bad, were internalized—brought into you—and formed the foundation of your own personality.
4. The more unpleasant experiences and emotions that you felt in early childhood were repressed and now are removed from your awareness. They make up the unconscious part of your personality.

When you choose a romantic partner and begin a relationship, your earliest interpersonal experiences are reactivated; that is, you start to reexperience the feeling states you had as a very young child. During the first few phases of your relationship, the feeling states you reexperience will all be positive. That's because you're idealizing the person you've chosen as a romantic partner, and your personality plays along so that you can build a strong bond. (This mirrors your early bonding with your parents.) It's as you progress into the

early- and late-reality phases, and eventually into the commitment phase, that you allow yourself to experience negative
feeling states. By now the proverbial bloom is off the rose,
and you're determining whether the positive feelings you as-
sociate with your partner outweigh the negatives: if so, the relationship can progress through commitment and possibly
into marriage.

That, in a nutshell, is the genesis of every romantic relationship you've had or will have. Understanding that genesis is a
powerful tool for making your relationship more rewarding
and fulfilling. The key is to create a knowledge base about the
personalities—yours and your partner's—involved in the relationship, which you do through
the processes of self-observation, observation of your partner, and communication. You watch. You reflect.
You talk. And, when you see the
need, you make course corrections;
you modify your behavior so as not
to inflict psychological pain on your
partner, and you ask them to do the
same for you.

> You watch. You
> reflect. You talk. And,
> when you see the
> need, you make
> course corrections.

Which, of course, is easier said than done. (A good dose
of patience and a quick reread of chapters 6, 7, and 8 can
help.) When you're in the thick of a romantic relationship, it
can be extremely difficult to be objective and follow princi-
ples of good, constructive relating. And since you and your
partner chose each other based on the mutual unconscious

perception that you could gratify each other's needs, any failure to do so by one of you is bound to create feelings of frustration (and deprivation!) in the other. Those negative feelings can make communication next to impossible.

If the negative feelings in your relationship start to outweigh the positive, and all attempts at communicating and relieving the strain seem to come to naught, it may be time to bring in a little outside help. Couples therapy is a process through which a trained psychologist can figure out where the breakdown in your pattern of relating is happening, explain that breakdown to you, and suggest steps that you and your partner can take to get your relationship back on track. What's critical to remember is that in couples therapy, *you're* not the patient, and neither is your partner: the relationship is the patient.

Should you take this step, here's what'll happen: your therapist will observe you and your partner to learn the ways in which your relationship is dysfunctional. He or she will also collect information about both of your families. Armed with all of this information, your therapist will help you and your partner understand each other's personality dynamics, and will also help you see what role each of you takes during conflicts. Your therapist will be a neutral observer, basically taking over the self-observation role that your problems have rendered too difficult for you to perform. Over time, your therapist will come up with strategies to help you both deal with problems as they arise. Most of all, the therapist will teach you both better communication skills. When therapy has been successful, you'll learn to reframe what you say to each other in ways that will provoke positive reactions . . . instead of provoking yet another fight.

One of the main functions of a couples therapist—and certainly the main function of this book—is to help you understand how the relationships of your childhood affect your adult romantic relationships.

But not *just* your adult romantic relationships. The truth is, while we've looked at committed love relationships on these pages, you're in the middle of dozens of other relationships that are also affected by that personality of yours, the one that was formed by your earliest interpersonal bonds. Chances are good that you're still in a parent-child relationship, and you're certainly in several friend-friend relationships. Perhaps you've got an employer-employee bond, or maybe a student-teacher one. You live every day of your life in these relationships.

And the success or failure of every single one of your relationships is determined by who you are as a person: the conscious and unconscious aspects of your personality, the kinds of feelings you bring out in others, your capacity to effectively communicate, and your ability to "tune in" to the needs of others (and fulfill those needs), all play a role in how you relate to the people in your life. The things that you've learned on these pages can all be applied, with a little bit of modification, to any of your relationships. (As can that stuff you wrote in your notebook. Just because you collected personal observations and reflections in order to understand your *romantic* relationship a bit better doesn't mean you can't also use that knowledge to help you deal with a parent, a coworker, or a tricky friendship.)

Forgive the clichéd reference to Shakespeare, but the guy had it right when he wrote that our faults lie "not in our stars, but in ourselves." It's because our *selves*—our personalities— are so intricately connected to the families in our past and have such a profound effect on the people in our present and the children we create, that we owe it to each other to work hard at communicating, loving, and relating.

Acknowledgments

Philip Van Munching
This time around, I'd like to express my thanks and love to:

Dave Spalthoff for his friendship, generosity, and near-perfect
24 attendance;
Tom Werner for his boundless enthusiasm and encouragement;
Steve Laico, Webmaster and Piano Man;
Maria Ciaravino for saying all the right things when she read
the first draft;
my folks, Peggy and Leo Van Munching, Jr., for having a
sense of humor about the title;
and Mary and David Solomon for opening their doors in cel-
ebration.

I am blessed with two brilliant, beautiful, and kind editors. (And a wife who begrudges me neither. *Man,* I'm lucky.) Elizabeth Beier at St. Martin's Press is responsible for just about anything and everything that works on these pages, and Liz Auran continues in her unpaid role as editrix/cheerleader. Bernie and I are in debt to you both.

In fact, Bernie and I owe a great deal to all the good folks at St. Martin's who've worked on this book, especially—and alphabetically—Courtney Fischer, Christina Harcar, John Murphy, Cara Petrus, Sally Richardson, Michelle Richter, Sabrina Soares Roberts, Frances Sayers, and Lisa Senz. John Sargent got the ball rolling on my last book, so I'm particularly glad to have done this one with his crew.

Thanks go, most of all, to Christina, Anna, and Maggie Van Munching. Elizabeth Beier loves it when I borrow lines from movies, so here's one more: You three make me want to be a better man.

Bernie Katz, Ph.D.

I'd like to acknowledge those people who have helped make me a better person by their presence in my world of relationships:

First, my children, Ellen and Steven, have enriched my life immeasurably with healthy doses of mutual love, devotion, pride, and respect. Beth, my stepdaughter, brings much joy and pleasure. Lon, my stepson, had wit, wisdom, and bravery that were never less than inspirational. His untimely passing has saddened us all.

After forty years of teaching, I have collegial relationships that have outlasted many marriages. I wish to thank my colleagues in the Psychology Department at NCC for their friendship, assistance, support, and camaraderie. Our bonds go far beyond the workplace; we are truly "family" to one another.

I would also like to acknowledge my friends of many years with whom I have shared our mutual triumphs and disappointments for their love, their laughter, and their consistency.

Finally, I offer my heartfelt thanks to my loving wife, Harriet, for all that she is and all that she does. Our love gets better with age, and our relationship continues to mature with increasing intimacy, commitment, and understanding.